City Family

Farm Family

By Roslyn Ross

The stories in this book are true.

They take place in the years 2013 and 2014.

1. Building

There was a family with a mama, a papa, and a little boy just under two-years-old named Anders. They were an adventurous family, but they had a big problem: they could not decide where to live.

Mama and Papa wanted to live in a giant city. They loved the idea of Anders growing up in a giant city, because children who grew up in giant cities were often savvy, street-smart, and competitive.

But Mama and Papa also wanted to live on a farm. They loved the idea of Anders growing up on a farm, because children who grew up on farms were often tough, healthy, and grounded.

Mama and Papa wanted to live in two places, and they wanted Anders to grow up in two places, so, they decided to do an experiment to see what it was like living in two places.

The giant city in which they decided to live was Los Angeles, California. Four million people live in Los Angeles, but unlike other giant cities like New York and London, filled with apartment buildings and skyscrapers, Los Angeles was more like one big sprawling suburb.

Mama and Papa bought a medium-sized house on Archwood Street in an area of Los Angeles called Tarzana. Their new house had a big backyard with ten fruit trees, two giant shade trees, a pool in which Anders could swim, room for Anders to ride his balance bike, and dirt in which Anders could dig.

Moving into the new house was a lot of work. First, Mama and Anders unpacked all the boxes. There were a lot. It took them almost a week just to take everything out of the boxes and arrange and rearrange the rooms, cupboards, and drawers to make their new home as organized as possible.

When that was done, Mama and Anders needed to go to many different furniture and home-decorating stores. Today they were going to one of Anders's favorite stores—Ikea.

Ikea was a huge store housed in a giant monstrosity of a building that took up as much space as a large city block. The building had almost no windows and was low to the ground for its size. The entire rectangular shape was painted in royal blue. Huge bright yellow letters spelled out its name. The style made Mama think of Legos—from the outside, the store looked like a giant Lego block.

When they walked inside the store a Swedish man, whose job it was to greet them, said, "Hi, welcome to Ikea."

"Thank you," said Mama.

"Thank you," said Anders.

"Do you want to take the stairs or the escalator today?" Mama asked. Anders chose the stairs, and up they went.

At the top of the stairs there was a cement path with large, yellow arrows showing visitors the way to go. The path was lined with rooms. First there were dozens of living rooms, then, farther down the path, there were dozens of bedrooms, then offices, kitchens, dining rooms, and bathrooms. Then there were entire apartments that visitors could enter and explore. It was like a series of adult-sized doll houses, all impeccably stylish.

Mama and Anders walked slowly down the path, marveling at all the things to see. Whenever Mama or Anders saw a room they liked, they left the path and explored that room for a while. It took almost two hours for them to walk the entire floor.

Eventually Mama found what she had come for—a tall, simple, white bookcase. She stared at it for a long time, envisioning how it would look in their new living room. Eventually she said, "Okay, I'm ready. Let's go get it!"

They took an elevator downstairs to the warehouse where customers went to get the furniture they had picked upstairs in the showrooms. Mama got a giant shopping cart. It was perfectly flat and low to the ground. Anders stood on it and practiced balancing while Mama pushed. Then he sat down, and Mama gave an extra hard push and let go of the cart! Anders squealed with delight.

"Whee!" he said. "Again!" So, Mama did it again and again.

Soon they were at the boxes of bookcases. Anders climbed off the cart. Mama, grunting and struggling, loaded a heavy, flat box as tall as she was, filled with all the pieces to make a bookcase, onto the cart. Anders helped Mama push the cart to the checkout line. They paid, and then it was time to figure out how to get the box into Mama's car. Again, Mama grunted and struggled, but she managed to get the box into the car.

Now it was time to go home, but Anders was not ready yet.

"Two more minutes," he said. He was climbing all over the car, experiencing the new spaces created by the giant box.

Mama smiled and sat down in the driver's seat. She took a book out of her purse and said, "Okay, tell me when you're ready." Mama always had a book in her purse for waiting times. Mama loved waiting times—she loved giving Anders the gift of all the time he needed to finish studying something, and, more than that, she loved taking a little break from the busy-ness of the day to read and learn something new herself.

In ten minutes or so, Anders said, "All done!" and climbed into his car seat. Mama put away her book, and strapped him in.

Soon Mama and Anders were home. Now it was Anders's favorite part of the day—it was time to build!

Mama and Anders opened the box and took out several large pieces of painted wood, one even bigger piece of carboard backing, some small nails, some wooden pegs, and two different types of screws. Anders inspected everything while Mama read the instructions.

"We need a flat-head screwdriver, a Phillips screwdriver, and a hammer to do this project," she said.

"Okay!" said Anders. He ran to his room. He brought back two toolboxes filled with a selection of tools. Then he searched through them for what they needed.

Mama pointed to the first step in the instructions. "We start with the wooden pegs." She showed Anders the holes into which the wooden pegs must go.

Anders grabbed his hammer. He had his very own metal hammer, the same kind of hammer a grownup might use. Anders had had a plastic hammer when he was a baby, but it had broken one day while he was hammering with it. Then Mama had gotten Anders a wooden child's hammer with which he practiced for quite some time, but eventually the head came off. Then Mama decided to get Anders a small, metal hammer. Anders had practiced hammering so much that he was able to use the metal hammer without hurting himself or the furniture.

Anders, one by one, put the wooden pegs in place and then hammered them into the board. Then it was time for step two. Anders screwed in many screws, and Mama went over them to make sure they were tight enough. Soon it was time to put the bookcase together. Mama had to do that part. But when she was done, Anders hammered all the little nails into the carboard backing. Finally, Mama stood the shelf up. It looked great!

"Never climb on this, Anders," she said, and showed him how easily it could fall over. "Ouch," she said.

"Ooouuuuch!" Anders said, understanding.

Mama started putting books onto the bookshelf. Anders got upset. He wanted to take the bookcase apart and put it together again!

"Oh honey," Mama said, "I wish I had time to do that with you, but I don't today."

Whenever Mama said "no" to Anders in one way, she tried to say "yes" in another way. Right now, Anders was feeling emotional, so Mama said "yes" in two ways. "We have to go to Ikea again soon to get a bed. That will be a big project! Do you want to go to Ikea again soon?"

"Yes," Anders said nodding.

"And right now, I need to be done putting furniture together, because I have a huuuuge cooking project I need to get to. Do you want to help me with my cooking project?"

"Yes," Anders said.

"Okay, let's put these books on the bookshelf super-fast, so we can get to the kitchen!" Mama said, starting to pile books onto the bookshelf as fast as she could. Anders loved doing things super-fast, and he couldn't wait to start the cooking project, so he got right to work putting books on the shelves he could reach.

Over the first six months that they lived in the Archwood Street house, Mama and Anders put together a king bedframe, a twin bedframe, two bedside tables, three desks, four bookcases, a dining room table, and six chairs. That is how Anders became such an expert with hammers and screwdrivers at such a young age that one day, while still a toddler, Mama woke up and found that Anders had removed two of the legs from the dining room table.

2.   Birthday

Now it was October 7th, Anders's birthday. Today he was two years old. He was an intelligent, independent, and enthusiastic little guy who could be reasoned with even when upset. Anders had never thrown a tantrum and rarely cried.

To celebrate his birthday, Mama, Papa, and Anders drove to the train station in Chatsworth and caught a train to downtown Los Angeles. Trains were Anders's current favorite thing, and Mama couldn't think of a better way to celebrate Anders's life than by doing his favorite thing.

The Chatsworth Amtrak Station, the train station nearest to their house on Archwood Street, was unimpressive. It was little more than a large, ugly parking lot next to some train tracks. It had a small, ugly building where train tickets used to be sold, but the building was currently unused except as a waiting room because train tickets were now sold by an ugly machine just a few feet from the train tracks. Mama had already purchased their tickets on the internet though, so they did not need to use the machine.

Papa held Anders in his arms. Anders looked around. He had played with toy trains, read realistic books about trains, watched YouTube videos of real trains, and visited a train museum full of trains that no longer worked, but he had never seen a real train roar down the tracks and stop in front of him in real life. Anders wanted Papa to put him down, so he could explore, but the train would arrive any minute.

"It's going to be very loud," Papa explained to Anders, "and more intense than you think. You might get scared, so please let me hold you until the train gets here. It will be here any minute."

"Okay," Anders said.

Two minutes later a blue and gray Amtrak train sped down the tracks and screeched to a halt just feet from the family. Anders was surprised by how much noise the train made. He covered his ears and hid his face in Papa's shoulder. When the train was fully stopped, and the doors opened. Anders watched as people got off. Then it was time to get on.

"Do you want to get on the train by yourself or do you want me to carry you?" Papa asked.

"Carry me!" Anders said.

Mama climbed aboard the train; Papa followed her with Anders in his arms. Then Anders was ready to be put down. He walked down the aisle of the train car, looking left and right excitedly.

"Let's sit here," Papa said, pointing to some empty seats. Papa, Mama, and Anders sat down. Anders sat in the seat closest to the window.

Soon the train started moving. Anders's eyes got wide. He looked out the window for a long time, entranced. When he was done looking out the window, he walked up and down the aisle of his train car and said "hi" to many old ladies who swooned happily at being greeted by him. Then the family went on an adventure to the snack car where they bought bubble waters and sat at a table looking out the window there.

It was only a thirty-minute ride to Union Station in downtown Los Angeles, so, soon, the family was getting off the train and walking through Union Station.

Union Station had been built a long time ago. It was grand. Its style was reminiscent of old Spanish style buildings—orange tile floors, white walls, and dark wood trimmings. Over time updates in different styles had marred the building's beauty some, making it look a little chaotic, but much of its old grandeur remained.

The family exited Union Station and took a taxi to a nearby restaurant called the Pacific Dining Car.

The restaurant was housed in several beautiful old train cars that no longer moved. The train cars had wood-paneled ceilings, lovely windows framed by dark red and green curtains, lush carpeting, and tables covered in white tablecloths and surrounded by chairs upholstered to match the curtains.

A waiter showed Mama, Papa, and Anders to their table. It was placed beneath an elegant pair of sconce lights with a window on either side. It was set with white and navy china, shiny and ornate silverware, simple water glasses, and fresh flowers. It was quite beautiful.

The family ordered an afternoon tea. Anders loved tea, and today he enjoyed many cups of it along with scones and lox sandwiches. He enjoyed the "Happy Birthday" song that Mama and Papa sang to him quietly. He enjoyed even more the candles that came in a slice of cheesecake at the end of the meal. Papa showed him how to blow out the candles. Anders loved that.

"Again!" he said. The waiter came by and relit the candles; as soon as Anders blew them out, he said, "Again!"

Mama laughed, "When we get home, we can play birthday candles as many times as you want," she said, "but it would be rude to keep asking the waiter to light the candles here."

Anders was exhausted from his big adventure and ready to go home, so the family got into a taxi and went back to Union Station. Anders was too tired to walk, so Papa carried him the whole way.

"My baby!" Papa said, loving this rare chance to hold his busy toddler. Anders slept for the whole train ride back to Chatsworth and the car ride home.

"Was it a good birthday?" Mama asked when they got back to their house and Anders was awake.

"Yes!" Anders said. "Blow out candles again?"

"Of course," Mama said, getting out a box of birthday candles.

Mama and Anders played birthday many times during the next few weeks. They put candles in whatever they happened to be eating—sweet potatoes, scrambled eggs, bread. Once they even tried to stick birthday candles into a piece of steak. That did not work very well.

3. Workbooks

The Archwood house had four bedrooms. One belonged to Anders. It was a simple room with plenty of open space where Anders could play. It had pale blue-green walls, bright blue-green curtains, and dark gray carpet. It had a lovely floor bed covered in a beautiful blue and green quilt made by Mama's grandmother, a large closet where all of Anders's clothes were stored, a small table with two chairs, and a child-sized set of shelves. One shelf was lined with baskets filled with toys – a basket of train toys, a basket of balls, and a basket of random toys. The other shelves were lined with various Montessori puzzles.

Mama sat in one of the small, child-sized chairs at the table. Anders sat in the other chair. On the table was something Anders had never seen before, a workbook.

"Now that you are two years old, I want to introduce you to a special kind of book," Mama said. "It is called a workbook. It was specifically designed to teach you something. It's not like a coloring book where you can pick any page to work on or color

16

whatever you want. This book has *directions*. It's a *class*."

"Ooooh," Anders said.

Mama opened the book to the first page. It had two crabs on it at opposite ends of the page. Between the two crabs were six rocks. "Can you draw a line from this crab to the other crab without crashing into any of the rocks?" Mama asked.

Anders picked up the pencil and drew a line from the crab at the top of the page to the crab at the bottom. He had to go around a few rocks to do this. Anders's pencil almost touched the rocks a few times. It was hard, but Anders liked the challenge. He finished the first page and wanted to do another.

On the next page Anders had to draw a line that followed a clear path from one bunny to another bunny.

"The goal," Mama explained, "is the same. Can you draw a line that stays on the path and doesn't crash into the side?"

Again, Anders focused and drew a line without touching the sides of the path, which, this time, were trees.

"These are called mazes," Mama said. "I see that you like them." Anders nodded. He finished the second page, the third page, and the fourth page. Then his hand started to get tired. He wasn't able to control his pencil as well anymore and couldn't stay on the path without crashing into the sides. "Your hand is too tired to do more," Mama said. "Let's stop now and do more of this tomorrow."

"No!" said Anders, grabbing the workbook protectively.

"You don't want to stop now," Mama said, "but your hand is too tired to keep working. This is not a coloring book. It's a special book. When your hand is too tired, it's time to stop. But you can color in a coloring book if you want."

"No coloring book," Anders said.

"Okay, no coloring book," Mama said.

Anders picked up his pencil. He wanted to keep working! Mama put her hand over his hand and said gently, "I can't let you keep working in this book. You are not able to do the lines now. This is a special book. If you do the pages incorrectly, you won't learn what this book has to teach and the book will be wasted. But I have two ideas so we can both get our needs met: I can draw you a maze on some paper or we could photocopy the next page of this book and you could do the photocopy."

"Photocopy," Anders said.

Mama photocopied the next page in the book. She made five copies. She gave them to Anders one at a time and, one at a time, he did them, but he couldn't do the maze without hitting the side. He was so disappointed and frustrated! He was telling his hand what to do and trying so hard, but his hand was not cooperating. He started to cry. Mama picked him up and carried him to the couch. They cuddled until Anders was done crying.

Then Mama said, "Your body just needs to rest. Rest is magical and fixes many problems. Let's rest here for a while, and when you are done resting, we can make pumpkin cookies." They cuddled on the couch for a few more minutes and then Anders, who was rarely upset for long, looked at Mama and smiled.

"Pumpkin cookies!" he said gleefully.

The next day, after Anders had had a good night's rest, he was able to do the fifth page of his workbook with ease.

4.   A Dream

After Anders took a long bath, Mama brushed and flossed his teeth. Then Anders put on a diaper and pajamas and got into bed.

Sometimes Anders slept in Mama and Papa's big bed. Sometimes he slept in his own little bed in his own room. Most of the time Mama and Papa had no opinion about where Anders should sleep because they loved sleeping with their little boy, but they got better sleep when he slept on his own. Mama and Papa liked getting better sleep, but they knew that childhood was short, and a time would come in not so very long that they would never get to sleep with their little boy again, so for now, they left the choice to Anders. If he wanted to sleep in his own room, that was great. And if he wanted to sleep with them, that was great too.

Tonight, Anders wanted to sleep with Mama and Papa, so he climbed into their big bed, and Mama turned out the lights. Now it was time to lie in bed and talk about their day. This evening Anders had some questions for Mama.

Anders asked, "Bees hungry?"

Mama answered, "Yes, I think so."

Anders asked, "Bees like scrambled eggs?"

Mama said, "I don't think so. You like scrambled eggs, but I think bees like the pollen in flowers."

Anders said, "Bees fly. Bzzzzzz. Ducks fly. Fish fly?"

Mama said, "No, fish don't fly. But they can jump very high."

Anders got excited. He said, "Fish jump. Jumpin'! Jumpin' fly. Fish jump fly!"

Mama agreed, "Yeah, fish do look like they're flying when they jump. You're thinking of the dolphin documentary you saw today."

Anders said, "Yes! Chickens fly?"

Mama said, "No, they don't, and it's tricky because they have wings just like ducks and the other birds, but chickens can only glide a little bit; they can't fly."

Anders said, "Horses. Horses jump. Hooooorrrrsses. Horses floss?"

Mama said, "Horses have teeth like us, but they don't floss."

Then Mama heard the heavy breathing of Anders fast asleep. She turned on her reading light and read until Papa came home. They talked quietly about their days for a few minutes, and then they went to sleep too.

In the morning, Papa woke up first and went to work. Mama read in bed until Anders woke up about thirty minutes later. While Mama was sitting in bed reading, and Anders was sleeping next to her, he started smiling a very big smile. Mama looked at him and thought that he looked so precious lying there smiling. She wondered what he was dreaming about and felt happy thinking that Anders was having a good dream. Maybe he was dreaming about puppies.

Then Anders started giggling. Now Mama really wanted to know what Anders was dreaming about. Maybe the puppies were licking his face! In his sleep Anders said, "Mama!" and kept giggling to himself with his eyes closed. Mama was dying to know what was going on in his dream. Then Anders said gleefully, "Mama farted! Biiiiiig fart!" He giggled some more and then his face relaxed, and he was once again sleeping peacefully.

Mama laughed quietly to herself. "Of course he was dreaming about farts and not puppies," she thought, shaking her head.

5.   Culture Club 101

"Want to go to Culture Club 101 with me?" Mama asked Anders.

"Yes!" Anders said.

They drove to Culture Club 101, an obscure little store that had just opened a few months before. It was a grocery store, but it was located in a small, one-bedroom house on a residential street. It was quite dark as the house didn't have many windows, but it was clean and well-kept, and, most importantly, the woman who owned the store, Elaina, was passionate about sourcing and cooking the healthiest food available.

Mama really wanted to provide her family with healthy food. She had taken a class on nutrition in college and had read hundreds of books on nutrition since then. She knew that eating food rich in vitamins and minerals was imperative for good health. Vitamins and minerals are the tools bodies use to grow bigger and stronger and to fix problems like cut fingers or virus attacks.

City Family Farm Family

After many years and extensive nutritional analysis, Mama had invented a dozen nutritionally perfect meals, meals that provided the eater with a 100% of each day's recommended allowance of every vitamin and mineral per two thousand calories. These meals were all high fat, featured traditional flavor combinations, and made without any processed ingredients.

It was a lot of work to cook everything from scratch, but the way of eating that Mama had found made her so healthy she could take care of sick people and not get sick herself. In the last ten years Mama had only gotten one cold.

When Papa met Mama seven years ago, he did not eat healthy foods. He got frequent colds, and his hair was falling out. But now Papa ate like Mama, so, like Mama, he never got sick, and his hair had even stopped falling out.

Anders had always eaten healthy foods and for that reason had never had a cold in his life. He had no idea what it was like to have a sore throat, a stuffy nose, a fever, a headache, or a stomach-ache, and

26

Mama had no idea what it was like to have a sick child.[1]

One day Mama learned that an organization called the Weston A. Price Foundation espoused eating in almost the exact same way many years of mathematical analysis of different meals had led Mama to eat. Culture Club 101 was a Weston A. Price store. Part of the Weston A. Price philosophy was to be vigilant about where food was sourced.

Knowing what to eat was only half the battle. Finding high-quality food to buy was the other half. In a book called *Real Food, Fake Food*[2] Mama had learned that there was a lot of fraud in the food industry. Mama learned, for example, that many bottles labeled "olive oil" were not olive oil at all, but rather soy oil, and many jars labeled "honey" were not honey, but rather corn syrup.

That's why Mama was so happy when Elaina opened Culture Club 101. Elaina only sold food from farms that she had visited. Elaina had pictures of every farm whose products she sold. If a farm used any form of unhealthy pesticide, even an unhealthy pesticide

---

[1] Anders got his first cold at seven years old. He is ten now and has only had a fever once in his life. He has never been on antibiotics.
[2] By Larry Olmsted

that was considered organic, she did not sell its produce. If a farm didn't raise healthy animals, she didn't sell its meat. The foods she cooked and sold in her store were always of the highest quality: none of her food items had sugar in them; if they had honey, it was raw and local, if they had grains, those grains were organic, whole grains that had been soured or sprouted. Mama loved shopping at Culture Club 101. She could happily put anything that looked tasty into her shopping cart and trust that it was good for her and her family.

Mama parked the car under a tree in front of Culture Club 101. She unbuckled Anders from his car seat and stood back. Anders liked to climb out all by himself.

"Hi Anders!" Elaina said from behind the counter after Mama and Anders entered the store. "Hi Roslyn, how are you guys today?"

After exchanging pleasantries Elaina told Mama and Anders about a new product she had just received: potato chips made by an Amish family in Ohio. The potatoes had been grown without chemicals and had been fried in lard from healthy pigs rather than unhealthy vegetable oils.

"Would you like a bag of the chips?" Mama asked Anders.

Anders had never had potato chips before, so Elaina opened a bag for him to sample. He tasted a few and found them salty, crunchy, and delicious, so Mama added a few bags to her basket. Then she and Anders went through everything in the little store. Whenever Mama's shopping basket was half-full, Anders ran it to the counter and emptied it there for Elaina to ring up and put into bags.

Anders ran baskets full of butter and many different types of raw cheeses. He lugged glass quarts of raw Jersey milk and several large bags of sprouted whole grain flour. He carried a basket of jars filled with soaked and sprouted nuts. He carried many baskets of eggs, heads, feet, backs, legs, livers, hearts, and thighs from chickens that roamed free and were never fed any soy or corn products. He carried baskets of rib eye steaks, briskets, ground beef, heart, liver, and tallow from cows that had only ever eaten grass, and baskets of lard, bacon, breakfast sausages, and bratwurst sausages from healthy pigs. He carried baskets of fermented condiments, vegetables, and lacto-fermented sodas. By the time they were done, Anders was exhausted.

"Anders, you are the best helper I have ever seen! You just worked so hard, and I am so impressed that I have to give you some ice cream," Elaina said. "It's made from raw cream, eggs, honey, and vanilla. It's the best ice cream you will ever taste in your life." Elaina gave Anders a small jar of vanilla ice cream, and he gobbled down the entire thing. "I think he liked it," Elaina said to Mama.

"Was it the best ice cream you have ever had in your life?" Mama asked.

"Yes," Anders said, nodding seriously.

Whenever they went to Culture Club 101 Mama felt happy and inspired.

"I love this place!" Mama said to Anders when they were back in the car, and she was driving home. "This is how I want life to be! I find this level of quality so inspiring!"

"Yes!" Anders said. "Inspiring!"

"We spend a lot of our money on food," Mama explained, "about twenty-five percent of our income. There is a saying that I really like that I learned from your Granny Garrett. It goes like this: *You either give your money to the grocer now or the doctor later.*"

Anders didn't respond. Mama thought maybe that was because he had never been to the doctor, so he had no idea what she was talking about, but when she looked in the mirror, she realized that Anders was fast asleep.

6.   Scrambled Eggs

Usually, Anders was the assistant chef in the kitchen. He mixed, poured, added, and sprinkled when Mama asked him to. But one day about two months after his second birthday, Anders decided he wanted to master cooking something all by himself—and for seventeen days in a row he made scrambled eggs and sausages for breakfast mostly by himself.

Mama had spent a lot of time with Anders in the kitchen and watched him make good decisions regarding his own safety. "Hot" was his first word. He was always careful not to touch hot pots and pans, and though he did sometimes get splattered with hot things, he had never burned himself. [3]

Today was the seventeenth day Anders was making scrambled eggs and he could do almost everything on his own. He pulled his kitchen stool to the counter near the stove. He climbed up on the stool.

_____

[3] Anders was also an only child at this point, which made it easy for Mama to monitor him while he was doing risky things.

32

Mama put a cast iron pan on the stove and turned on the heat.

Anders dug some butter out of the tub and put it onto the pan to melt. He used a lot of butter, so that the eggs would not stick.

While the butter was melting Anders cracked eggs into a bowl. Then he spent a minute getting two pieces of shell out of the bowl. When there were no more shell pieces, Anders beat the eggs with a fork. He looked at the pan. The butter was melted and had little bubbles.

"Ready!" Anders said, and he poured the eggs into the pan. With his small spatula, he scraped the bottom of the pan.

Now it was time to add the sausages to the other pan. Because Anders's family bought heritage pork products, the sausage and bacon were much fattier than modern breeds. If Mama cooked just four slices of heritage-breed bacon from Culture Club 101, for example, she would get about a third of a cup of bacon grease leftover in the pan. If she cooked an entire package of bacon from a regular grocery store, she would be lucky to get a teaspoon of bacon grease.

The only downside to this fattier pork was that anyone too close to the cooking sausage got splattered with hot grease.

    To protect Anders from getting splattered, Mama always placed the sausage pan on the burner on the back corner of the stove. There was no way Anders, who was only thirty-two inches tall, could reach a pan on the back corner of the stove, so, when Anders first started making breakfast, he cooked the eggs, and Mama cooked the sausages. But Anders, wanting to do everything by himself, had realized that he could cook the sausages—by tossing them gently into the pan from where he stood. Mama resisted this idea at first as she did not think two-year-olds could aim that well, but Anders showed her that he could consistently toss the sausages into the pan without missing, which is what happened today—both sausages landed right where Anders wanted them.

When the eggs and the sausages were done cooking, it was time to put them on plates and take them to the table. Anders used his spatula to put the eggs on a plate. Mama added the sausages since he couldn't reach.

Then Anders climbed down from his stool and Mama handed him the plates. Anders brought the plates to the table, carrying them carefully to make sure nothing spilled. Then he came back, and Mama handed him silverware, which he also brought to the table. On his third trip he carried two cups of milk. Then it was time to sit down and eat.

Anders took a pinch of salt and a pinch of pepper and sprinkled them on top of his eggs.

"Will you put some on mine too?" Mama asked.

"Course," Anders said.

He sprinkled salt and pepper on Mama's eggs.

"Well, Anders, thank you for this breakfast. You have worked hard to learn how to do this," Mama said. "Remember when you first tried cracking eggs—how hard it was to get them to open? And now that you have practiced so much, it's easy!"

"Yes!" Anders said, immensely proud of himself.

Now that Anders had mastered cooking scrambled eggs all by himself, he took a break from making them for a long time. Mama was relieved. She loved scrambled eggs, but eating them seventeen days in a row had made her a little tired of them.

7. Big Noise

One day a well-meaning friend gave Anders a little drum and two drumsticks. Anders was happy about this. He loved banging on his drum! It made such big noises! Mama, on the other hand, did not enjoy it when Anders made big noises on his drum. It hurt her ears. Mama wondered if the noises were too loud for Anders's ears as well.

Mama searched the internet for how to measure the loudness of a sound. Sound, she learned, is measured in decibels, and sounds over 85 decibels were too loud and could cause permanent damage to people's ears. Mama found out there were apps she could download to her phone that would tell her how many decibels a sound was. So, she looked for the app with the best reviews, and downloaded it.

Mama went to where Anders was playing with his drum and noted that the sound was ninety-five decibels.

"Anders, I need to talk to you about something important," Mama said.

"Do you remember when we visited Grandpa, and he could not hear you well, so he kept asking you to repeat what you said? He kept saying, 'What?'"

Anders remembered. It had been frustrating to communicate with Grandpa because Grandpa could not hear well.

"His ears didn't work well because he damaged them by listening to noises that were too loud when he was young. I just measured how loud the noise on this drum is, and it is too loud. Look."

Mama showed Anders the decibel meter on her phone.

"Do you see that while I talk, this little arm right here changes? When I talk it goes here, to fifty-five, which is fine. Do you see these numbers over here to the right? These numbers are in red to warn us of danger because when a sound is that loud, it hurts our ears. Watch where the arm goes when I bang on your drum."

Mama gave the drum a good bang. The arm on the meter went into the red zone. Anders's eyes got big. He looked at Mama.

"It's too loud," she said. "I don't want to have problems with my ears when I am older. Do you want problems with your ears?"

"Nooooooooo," Anders said, shaking his head.

"Me neither. I like having my ears work well. I am going to buy some special earmuffs to protect your ears while you play with your drum. So today, I need to take the drum and put it away until the earmuffs get here."

Anders was sad. He really wanted to keep banging on his drum, but he understood why he couldn't. Mama put the drum away. Then Mama and Anders did a big sound-measuring project. They went all over the house with the decibel meter and measured how noisy their machines were—the air conditioner, the vacuum, and the blender.

"I can't believe I never did this before!" Mama said. "I am damaging my ears a little every day, and I didn't even realize it! Anders, I am not allowed to use the blender anymore until the earmuffs come."

"Okay!" Anders said.

"Will you remind me if I forget?" Mama asked.

"Yes!" Anders said. Anders had an excellent memory and loved it when Mama gave him special jobs like that.

A few days later three pairs of earmuffs arrived, one for Mama, one for Papa, and one for Anders. Now they could all put on their earmuffs, and Anders could bang away on his drum. Papa put a hook near the blender, so that Mama's earmuffs could hang there and always be available when she needed to blend something. [4]

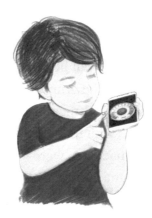

---

[4] Special note for those old enough to read: I do not think it is right to lie to children. However, parents, myself included, do not appreciate books that give their children bad ideas. So, in an effort to be respectful to parents, I turned the pots and pans in the kitchen with which Anders actually made loud noises into a drum set, so that young children who heard this story would not immediately head to the kitchen and bang on pots and pans. In an effort to be honest with children, however, I include this footnote, so that those old enough to read know the true story—those children old enough to read are also old enough to know better than to immitate every behavior that they read about.

8.   The Solstice

Now it was the winter solstice, the shortest day of the year. Mama, Papa, and Anders were going spend the entire day preparing for dinner that night. Twelve friends were coming over to join them for a feast of salad, short ribs, mashed potatoes, homemade bread, sticky toffee puddings, and vanilla ice cream.

Though Anders took breaks throughout the day to play outside, he spent most of the day chopping for Mama. There was a lot of chopping to be done, and Anders loved chopping.

Mama had a chopping tool that looked like a rectangular box with a metal grate across the top. The metal grate was made up of small squares. On top of the metal grate was a lid to the box. To use the chopper, Anders would take pieces of sliced vegetables and lay them on the grate. When the lid closed over the grate, the vegetable would be forced through the grate and fall into the box in nice, little squares. Anders was not strong enough to close the lid of the box with his hands, but he had figured out that if he closed it as far as he could with his hands and then stomped on it with his foot, he could get the lid closed all the way. This was great fun for Anders and helpful for Mama.

At five in the afternoon, it began to get dark. Mama told Anders he could plug in the lights on the Christmas tree, but that those were the only electric lights they would use today. Mama got out a box of beeswax candles. She lit them all and placed them around the kitchen and dining area. It looked magical.

"Mmmmmm," Anders said, smelling the candles.

"They smell like honey," Mama said. "Don't try to eat them though. They smell nice, but they are not tasty."

"Yuck," Anders said.

"That's right," Mama said. "Do you and Papa want to light the fire while I set the table?"

It was not cold. After all, they were in Los Angeles. But their house had a real, wood-burning fireplace, and Mama wanted to use it.

Anders and Papa crumpled junk mail into balls and threw the balls into the fireplace. That was great fun. Then, they went outside to gather kindling—small sticks that would help get the fire burning. Papa showed Anders how to arrange the kindling on top of the junk mail. Anders enjoyed this and spent a long time arranging and rearranging the little sticks. Then they went to the wood pile and brought in big pieces of firewood. Anders was excited to find he could carry large pieces all by himself, so he brought in lots of extra pieces. They put the big pieces on top of the kindling and then the fire was ready to light.

Papa lit the junk mail at the bottom. The fire from the burning paper made the small sticks catch on fire, and the fire from the small sticks made the bigger pieces of wood catch on fire. The whole process was mesmerizing to watch.

Mama finished setting the table and put on some holiday music.

"Everything is ready," Mama said. "The guests will be here soon."

Anders examined the beautiful table. There were flowers in the middle, bottles of wine, pitchers of water, and lit candles. At each chair there was a shiny silver charger, a white dinner plate with a matching salad plate on top, a water glass and a wine glass, a fork, salad fork, knife, and dessert spoon, and a bread plate with a butter knife. There were scarlet-red dinner napkins with shiny silver napkin rings in the center of each dinner plate.

"Doesn't it look glorious?" Mama asked.

"Yes," Anders said, but he had an idea of how to make it even better. He went to his room and got his toolbox. He placed hammers, screwdrivers, and nails around the table.

"More glorious now," Anders said, smiling at his work.

Soon their friends began to arrive. Anders's babysitter arrived too and asked if he wanted to go play in the garage. Anders most certainly did, but he needed his hammers and screwdrivers, so he removed them from the table.

Mama was sad to see the hammers and screwdrivers go. She loved those decorations. She loved that Anders had had an opinion about the decorating and had added his own personal touch to the table. She loved those little things about a home that said, "A child lives here." She also thought the guests would have been entertained by the decorations—how many beautifully set dinner tables had hammers and screwdrivers as part of the decorating theme? But Anders had more important uses for the tools now. He carried them to the garage, so that he and the other children who had arrived could use them.

While the grownups ate and talked for hours, the kids played in the garage. There was a piece of drywall that was easy for the children to hammer nails into. Five children aged two to four worked for hours, hammering many nails into the drywall. Then they removed the nails and hammered them in again into new places. They screwed in many screws as well.

At the end of the evening the adults were invited to see the work the children had done. The number of nails and screws in the drywall was impressive, as were the newfound skills of the children who had never used hammers or screwdrivers before. The children were pleased with themselves.

"This is crazy," one of the guests, Priscilla, said, shocked that the kids had enjoyed themselves so much and been kept busy for so long with just some hammers, screwdrivers, nails, screws, and drywall. "What made you decide to do this instead of, say, put on a movie?"

"Anders said he wanted a hammering party," Mama said. "I figured they could always watch a movie if they got bored."

"No movies! Boooo!" cried Anders. "Hammering parties!"

"Hammering parties!" chimed in the other children.

"I'm definitely going to do this," Priscilla said. "I would much rather the kids spend an evening developing a new skill instead of sitting around watching a movie."

"Yay!" cried Priscilla's children.

"I think children, in general, prefer that too," Mama said. "They love developing new skills, especially if they are real skills. I don't think a basket of pretend tools would have kept them busy for more than twenty minutes."

"Totally," said Priscilla.

"Hammering parties!" said the children.

9.   Traveling

Now the family had lived in the giant city of Los Angeles for six months. It was time for the family to start their experiment of living in two places. It was time to head to a farm.

The farm where they decided to live was in a remote area of Nicaragua, a small country in Central America. Papa thought that if they were going to live in two places, it would be especially fun, adventurous, and interesting if those two places were in two different countries with two different cultures and two different languages. In Nicaragua the main language is Spanish. This would be hard for Mama and Papa, but Anders would be bilingual. Mama and Papa loved that idea.

Papa also wanted their farm to be in Nicaragua because one of Papa's best friends from college, Ken, was from Nicaragua. Mama wasn't a big fan of the heat, but she liked Ken, and she liked the things he had to say about Nicaragua, so she agreed to give it a try.

With Ken's help, Papa found a farm to buy in Nicaragua. Well, it wasn't a farm yet, right now it was just thirty acres of land. The family would have to turn the raw land into a farm. That would be part of the adventure.

Today was the traveling day. Anders loved traveling. He loved every part of it. He loved packing things in suitcases—he had his own little suitcase that he packed himself with his favorite toys. He rolled it behind him at the airport. He loved standing in line. There were so many interesting things to see and so many interesting people to meet. Anders was outgoing and generally made friends with whomever happened to be standing in line in front of him and behind him.

Anders loved escalators. He didn't like to ride them yet; he preferred the stairs. Mama and Papa also preferred the stairs, so they all took the stairs together, but whenever they saw an escalator, they would stop, so that Anders could study it for a while. Anders loved the big windows at the airport with all the planes outside to see. He loved sitting down by the big windows and watching the planes. He rarely even opened his suitcase of toys before the flight—looking out the windows took up all the waiting time.

The best part about going to the airport, though, was when it was time to get on the plane. Anders liked to hold his boarding pass himself and give it to the flight attendant. He loved walking down the long hallways to the plane and getting on the plane.

He always said, "Hi!" to the flight attendants and to many passengers as he walked down the aisle to his seat. Usually, people found this charming and smiled at him, but they rarely talked to him. Today was different. Today they were flying on Avianca Airlines. Today when he greeted the flight attendants, they took a moment to talk to him. They told him he was *muy lindo*[5] and gave him things—crackers and a pin with wings.

As Anders walked down the aisle to his seat, greeting people as he always did, they didn't just smile in return; they talked to him. Mama and Papa were a little anxious about how long it was taking to get to their seats, and though they encouraged Anders to stop talking to people and keep going, no one else seemed to be concerned—not even the flight attendants.

When Anders got into his seat the man in the seat in front of him and the woman in the seat behind him immediately started talking to him. Mama could not believe how friendly everyone was.

The friendliness continued for the entire six-hour flight. The flight attendants stopped by every half hour or so to talk to Anders and bring him something interesting. They brought him water, juice, extra

---

[5] handsome

snacks, and anything else they thought he might like, like straws and paper napkins. One time they even brought him a toy airplane that said Avianca on it!

The woman in the seat behind Anders talked to him a lot and played peek-a-boo with him throughout the flight. The man in the seat in front of him talked to him and played peek-a-boo with him too. When Anders got tired of sitting and decided to go for a walk down the aisle of the plane, he made friends with a lady who had an interesting-looking purse in her lap. Then Anders, who was only three months passed his second birthday and still learning the rules of ownership, tried to take her purse.

She did not get mad at all; she smiled at him and said, "Oh, no, no, no, this is mine. But I can show you what is inside." She started removing items from her purse one by one and showing them to Anders.

Mama and Papa, who were watching the whole thing looked at each other incredulously.

"We should get him; he's driving her crazy," Papa said.

"I don't know," Mama said. "Is it possible that when Americans are being kind, they tolerate toddlers on planes but that Nicaraguans . . . genuinely like them? I don't understand what is going on either, but no one seems upset."

Mama went up to the woman talking to Anders. "Excuse me, is he bothering you?" Mama asked.

"No, not at all. This is my new friend!" the woman said. Mama went back to her seat.

In a little while Anders was done talking to the woman with the interesting purse and decided to keep going down the aisle of the plane, but a man stopped him and said, "Your mom and dad are back that way." Anders looked where the man was pointing and headed back to his mom and dad.

"Did you see that?" Papa asked. "Americans are basically afraid to talk to other people's kids."

"This is so interesting," Mama said. "When we were flying to Alabama for the wedding last summer, Anders did the same thing—he tried to take some woman's purse—and she didn't even look at him, she just looked immediately at me like she was being attacked, and I needed to do something."

Mama and Papa were soon to find out that it wasn't just the people on the airplane who would be this way with Anders. It was everyone at the hotel, at the restaurants, at the malls; it was the neighbors at the farm—it was part of the culture in Nicaragua.

10. Heatstroke

By the time they arrived in Managua, the capital of Nicaragua, it was late at night. Ken, Papa's friend who lived there, had told them to stay at a hotel near the airport called Camino Real. He told them to guard their bags carefully at the airport and only get into a van that said Camino Real on it. Ken said that if the van wasn't there, they needed to call their hotel and wait for it. He said to never get into a taxi at the airport. Nicaragua was a Third World country, and the rules of safety were different from what Mama and Papa were used to, so they needed lots of advice. As long as they followed his advice, Ken assured them, they would be safe.

There were no problems, though. The van from their hotel was waiting for them when they got outside. The driver greeted them, loaded their bags, and took them straight to the hotel. A uniformed bellman stood outside the hotel. In the United States only expensive and fancy hotels have bellmen. In Nicaragua, even the plain ones do. Mama loved this.

The bellman took their bags from the van to the lobby, where he stood with them the entire time Mama and Papa checked in. Anders made friends with the bellman, who let him help push the luggage cart.

In the morning, Ken met them for breakfast. He was impeccably dressed (as he always was) and Mama admired his effortless manners. He brought a pick-up truck for the family to use during their stay. Anders was super excited—he had never ridden in a truck before! They loaded their luggage into the back of the pickup truck. Ken showed them how to cover it with a tarp and tie it down. "If you don't cover it, it could get wet if it starts raining, and if you don't tie it down, someone could hop into the back of your truck and grab one of the suitcases when you stop at a stop sign or a red light."

After they tied down the luggage – with Anders's help – and covered it with tarps, Ken said goodbye. It was time to go to the farm. The drive would take more than two hours.

When Mama first stepped out of the air-conditioned hotel and into the hot, humid air outside, she felt like she had been punched in the stomach.

"Wow, I am really hating the heat a lot more than I thought I would," she said.

Papa, Mama, and Anders got into the truck and Papa started driving. They put the windows down because the truck's air conditioner was broken. About fifteen minutes into the drive Mama felt like she was going crazy from her hatred of the heat. She knew that what was hitting her in the face was only the hot wind, but it hurt as if she were being slapped. Her heart was beating fast. She felt disoriented, dizzy, and angry.

Usually, she was excited and happy to explore new places, so she did not know what was wrong. She began to cry, but no tears came out. Usually when she cried, Mama felt better right away, but this time she felt like she couldn't breathe.

Papa heard Mama taking controlled breaths and put his arm around her.

"Wow, you feel really hot!" he commented. Mama wanted to tell him how uncomfortable she felt but talking just seemed too exhausting. So, Mama laid her head back against the seat and closed her eyes. She felt tired and thought that she would take a nap. But just as she was about to pass out, it suddenly occurred to her that she might be having heatstroke. It was first thing in the morning; there was no reason she should be this tired. Mama realized she hadn't had a lot of water in the last two days. She hadn't even gone pee that entire day so far and had gone maybe only once the day before.

Mama used her phone to look up "heatstroke," and it described exactly what was going on with her. She immediately drank some water and dumped an entire bottle of water on her head, and in breathless spurts she told Papa to get her into a cool room as quickly as possible.

Papa stopped at the next gas station. It was exactly what Mama needed. It was air conditioned inside and had a restaurant area with tables and chairs where she could sit down.

Mama drank more water and Gatorade (a terrible mistake, but she didn't know that then) and held a bag of ice on her lap until she felt better. After twenty minutes had passed, Mama felt completely fine. Papa touched Mama's head again and said she did not feel hot anymore. Anders touched Mama's head too and agreed with Papa.

When Mama stepped out of the air-conditioned gas station and into the outside air, this time the air just felt hot and humid. This time when she rode in the truck with the window down, the wind just felt like wind. She didn't feel angry anymore. Now she just felt excited! And of course, relieved that she had realized she was having heatstroke in time. If she hadn't realized it and had fallen asleep, she could have died.

11. The Farm

Now that Mama was feeling better, she started noticing where she was. Nicaragua was a lot less green than she had imagined, because it was January, the beginning of their dry season. The countryside was mostly rolling hills. There were trees, but most were small and shrubby. Every now and then they passed by a group of shacks on the side of the road. The shacks were built of old, unpainted wood and had rusty metal roofs. Outside, children stood around listlessly. Men and women, dressed in jeans and tank tops or T-shirts, sat in inactivity. No one she saw was smiling or moving very fast. There was an endless amount of trash on the side of the road.

They drove by a few unpainted cement homes shaped like boxes. These homes had metal roofs and bars over the windows and doors. There were a lot of animals to see: chickens, horses, cows, goats, and dogs. Anders loved seeing all the animals, but Mama thought they looked thin and unhealthy.

The highway was nice, perfectly smooth, and black. It was only two years old. Before it was built the only roads into this area of Nicaragua had been dirt roads.

"I was expecting more … rainforest," Mama said.

"There was rainforest here eighty years ago," Papa said. "But they cleared it to make room for cattle. Without the trees, the area has become quite dry and much hotter. The cattle industry is moving to the mountains now, where it is cooler. This land is pretty destroyed, so the prices are low. We will fix our land and make it healthy again. And we will plant trees, and that will lower the temperature and bring rain."

After another hour and a half in the car Papa turned off the highway. The dirt driveway he turned onto was barely visible. Overgrown shrubs covered the ground on both sides of it. Soon a building came into view, and Papa parked the car.

"Okay, we're here!" Papa said.

Mama and Anders got out and looked around. Short, angular, shrubby trees called *guasimos* surrounded the area. They provided little shade. There were four buildings: a small, dark wooden shack with a rusty metal roof that stood at the top of a small hill; a small cement box of a building with a red metal roof; a cement building shaped like an "L" with four tiny rooms and a red metal roof; and the rancho, a large wooden building open on one side, hastily built with spaces between the boards and spiderwebs everywhere. The rancho had a bathroom on one side with a toilet stall where a wooden toilet seat sat on top of a five-gallon bucket. A bucket of sawdust sat next to it.

"What do you think?" Papa said.

"The air smells like it's chemical-free," Mama said.

"That bad, huh?" Papa said, smiling.

"I am a little overwhelmed by the ugliness of it all," Mama said honestly.

Papa nodded. He had known that's what Mama would say. "That's why I need you here," he said.

He showed Mama and Anders to the room they would share. It was tiny, barely big enough for a twin-sized bed. There wasn't enough room for Papa to sleep there too, so he would sleep in a cot in the rancho. Anders and Mama's room was box shaped; the walls, ceiling and floor were unpainted cement. All day long cement dust from the walls would gather on their bed, and all day long Mama would shake it off. The room had two screen windows—ill-fitting screens nailed into rough, moldy wood frames. There was no furniture in the room except a rough wooden bed frame and a cheap cushion for a mattress. There were two pillows on the bed. The pillows and the cushion were covered in scratchy polyester sheets so thin you could see right through the fabric. When Mama lay down on the pillow, it smelled like mold, so she looked under the pillowcase and, sure enough, the pillows were moldy.

"Just remember," Papa said, "this is the worst it will ever be. It will only get better." Just then an ant bit Mama's foot.

"OW!" Mama said, rubbing her foot.

Every minute at the farm for the next ten days was torture for Mama, but Anders loved it. Anders generally loved everything all the time, but he especially loved the farm. In Los Angeles most days it was just Mama and him. The farm had Nate, the farm manager, who lived there, and family friends that had decided to join the family for the trip. The friends that came were Nathaniel, Andrew, Marianna and Marianna's two young sons Michael and Daniel. There were also neighbors who stopped by to meet the crazy gringos. They often rode in on horses.

Papa also loved the farm. He felt relaxed.

"With no internet or television, my life comes into focus," he said. "Email, Facebook, the news—they're just distractions. Here at the farm, I don't know, maybe it's the darkness, but I sleep better than I ever have in my whole life."

Papa had vivid dreams all night long and woke up remembering all of them, which he loved. He also loved working outside. He loved tramping through the jungle shrubs and getting exercise all day. He was excited to solve immediate and concrete problems like building the water system and running power lines. He said being at the farm made him feel alive in a way that he never felt when he was living in the city.

"It's time for lunch," Papa said.

Everyone at the farm gathered into a group and walked down the driveway, and then out the barbed-wire gate to the highway. They walked down the side of the road in the hot sun to their nearest neighbor's house. Her name was Lillian.

Lillian had a small store where she sold beer, coffee, chips, candy, and other items the farming families in the neighborhood might want. She lived with her mother, her brother Trinio, Trinio's wife Mildre, and their two children, Alisa and José.

Lillian had agreed to provide lunch and dinner for the group during their two-week stay for a fee, and though Papa had offered her quite a bit of extra money, she absolutely refused to provide breakfast as well, saying it would be too much work. This was common in Nicaragua and was interesting to Mama and Papa. Many of the people lived in Third World poverty, yet they were usually uninterested in extra work. Mama and Papa did not know why this was, but a few years later one of their workers explained to them that he shared a home with thirty other family members. They lived in a large group, and no one got to keep his wages for himself. All the money any individual made was put into the common household pool. Because of this, no one wanted to work.

Everyone just wanted to take his turn not working and be supported by other members of the household.

Mama asked what would happen if everyone in the family decided to work hard and make money, so that the whole family could become wealthier. The man said that that would not work because as soon as the family had money, extended family members would start showing up to live with them and be supported by them.

"If all thirty people in the household were working, three hundred cousins would show up within a year," he explained.

Mama and Papa did not know if this family-level socialism explained the poverty they saw throughout Nicaragua, but it offered some insight as to why an impoverished person like Lillian might be uninterested in extra work.

Lillian's home was made up of many separate shacks, all made from rough wood and all with rusted metal roofs, serving different purposes. Lillian had electricity in only one of the buildings, a one-room building that served as the living and dining area. She had an old television there that was on day and night. This was where the grandmother and young children sat most of the day. This was also the room where she served lunch to Papa, Mama, Anders, and their friends.

Enough plastic chairs for everyone were arranged around two folding tables. The tables were neatly set with plastic tablecloths, paper napkins, foam plates, and plastic cups.

Lillian cooked in a separate shack nearby. She used water from a small well on her property and cooked everything over an open fire. For lunch she served beans and rice (called *gallo pinto*), freshly made thick corn tortillas, juice, and coffee. For dinner she served gallo pinto with *crema*, a soured cream she made each week; thick corn tortillas; eggs, chicken, or cheese; and juice. This is what was for lunch and dinner every day, without exception. All the family's neighbors in Nicaragua ate this basic meal three times a day. Though the food was boring, it was also tasty.

"I cannot get over how good things taste when they are cooked over an open fire!" Mama said. "The smoke flavor adds so much to the dish. You don't even need salt or spices on the rice and beans, just the smoke flavor."

"So tasty!" said Anders.

While they were eating, a dancing show came on the television and the two-year-old, Alina, got up and danced like the people on the screen. She mimicked them with a precision that was surprising to Mama, who had never seen a toddler dance that well before. Anders got up to dance too and so did Michael and Daniel. It wasn't long before the adults joined in, too. They laughed and had a great time.

12. Hormigas

At the farm there were bugs everywhere. There were flies, mosquitos, midges, and ticks. There were small, black bees that built nests that looked like mud pies; giant, black bumble bees; and wasps of every size. There were grasshoppers that were half an inch long, grasshoppers that were three inches long, and grasshoppers of every size in between. There were beetles many shapes, sizes, and colors that wandered the patios and in and out of rooms at will. There were large, brown spiders that could jump fifteen feet in a single leap! There were large, red spiders with orange and yellow spots that lived in the trees. There were scorpions, tarantulas, and whip spiders that skulked in dark places. At night, when Mama tried to read with a headlamp, there were so many moths that swirled around her forehead that she had to stop reading. The screen windows did not keep the bugs out at all.

The insect that ruled the farm was the ants. There were many different types, and each had its own name in Spanish: *hormigones,* a red fire ant whose sting hurt worse than a bee sting; *hormigas rojas,* tiny red ants that found their way into every glass of water; *guerras*, large black army ants that marched across the jungle in hoards devouring everything in their path; *hormigas*, small black ants that, if they got on you, stung you immediately and left an itchy bump, and *san popos*, leaf-cutter ants. These were the kings of the ants, the ants who the other ants feared, and the main enemy of farmers. They could cut or bite you and had a sting even worse than the hormigones'. The most annoying ants to Anders though were the hormigas because they were everywhere. It was impossible to walk from the fourplex to the rancho without getting stung by one.

One evening Mama and Anders watched two ants take down a large beetle. The ants were tiny, about the size of the beetle's leg. But they grabbed that beetle and dragged it off!

Mama had packed bags of nuts and dried fruit for Anders to snack on. They were unopened, airtight bags, sealed in plastic. But somehow ants got inside every single bag. Were the bags faulty? Did the ants make holes? Mama had no idea and was not able to figure out how the ants got into the bags.

One day, Papa, Mama, and Anders were walking to the rancho and every inch of the walkway––and one entire wall of the rancho—was covered in army ants. It looked like a plague, right out of a horror movie.

"What do we do?" Mama said.

"Nothing," said Nate, who was nearby. "They'll be gone in thirty minutes. They're just moving."

Mama, Anders, and Papa sat down to watch the ant swarm do its thing. Suddenly, a large scorpion jumped out from the floorboards of the rancho and started running for its life, running from the ants. Then spiders came out of the floorboards, large hairy jumping spiders, and huge black whip spiders. All of them ran from the ants. Some of the spiders got away, some were swallowed by the horde.

"It's uh, nice getting a show of all the spiders living beneath the floorboards where I sleep…." Papa said. Mama was horrified.

"I was stung by a scorpion when I was fifteen," she said. "It's painful."

"What's that, Roz? You don't like scorpions?" said Nate. He stamped his heavy boot on the fleeing scorpion. "It's dead."

"Thanks, Nate," Mama said, appreciating Nate's enthusiasm and permanent good attitude. "Can that be our policy on scorpions right now? Because Anders is so young?"

"Sure thing," said Nate. "I've been stung a couple times, though, and I don't think these scorpions are as bad as the ones in the U.S. It's like a bee sting when they get you. We need to get some chickens. They'll love all these bugs."

"Yes. We need chickens. And cows," Mama said.

"And pigs and goats and sheep," added Anders.

"And a garden, and a well, and Wi-Fi, and a kitchen…." Mama said.

Nate was right about the ants. Within thirty minutes, the swarm was gone. But the ants remained ever present, always ready to attack any fallen fellow bug and always ready to bite a foot that stood too long in the dirt.

The ants were the only thing Anders did not love about the farm. First, because they were the reason he had no snacks, and second, because they bit him all the time. "Hormigas" was Anders's first Spanish word.

One day, Anders was squatting near a pile of dirt and digging when he felt a sting on his arm, and then another sting on his back … and his neck … and his legs. There were so many stings! Anders began crying and ran to Mama screaming, "HORMIGAS!"

Mama saw that he was covered in ants. She ripped off his shirt and pants—getting stung herself, but she didn't let that distract her—and plunked him down into a five-gallon bucket of water. This got the hormigas off him, but he was covered in red bites.

"He looks like he has the measles!" Mama told Papa.

"Maybe this is a mistake," Papa said.

"Mother Nature is terrifying," Mama said. "I totally get the mentality of the pioneers now. The heat, the bugs. We need water. We need to grow food. Wrenching a life from raw land is so hard. I totally get it now. It is a war! When I was a kid, we used to sing a song that went, 'The earth is our mother, she will take care of us.' What a lie! It's more like Mother Nature wants to *kill* you!"

Papa laughed. "In Los Angeles we have to worry about all the chemicals and radiation we're being exposed to that could add up to cancer one day. The bug bites will go away."

Mama nodded and took Papa's hand. "They will. But they are not the dream. I'm not worried though. We're problem solvers; we will figure it out."

13. Potty Training

Now they were back in Los Angeles. It was February. Mama noticed that Anders could pull his pants down all by himself.

Mama said, "Anders, I notice that you can pull your pants down all by yourself. That means that maybe you are ready to use the toilet instead of wearing diapers. Would you like to do that—stop wearing diapers and use the toilet?"

"No," Anders said.

"Okay," Mama said. "Maybe when you are a little bit older you will be ready." Mama did not put any pressure on Anders to use the toilet, but she did want him to know where she stood on the matter, so she added, "It will be exciting for me when you use the toilet instead of wearing diapers. You will save your family a lot of money! Did you know that we have to buy every diaper that you wear? And every single one of those diapers costs money?"

"Oh," Anders said seriously.

"If you want," Mama said, "you could try running around naked in the backyard. That will make potty-training easier when you decide you are ready for it." Anders loved this idea and for the next few months he spent a considerable amount time of time running around naked outside. He learned quickly to control his pee and to squat to poop.

In March Mama noticed that Anders could not only pull his pants down all by himself, but he could pull them back up too, so she decided to ask again.

"Anders," she said, "I am noticing that you can pull your pants down *and* back up! I don't think you were ready to use the toilet before because you could not pull your pants back up yet, but now you can. Now, I think you may be ready. Would you like to stop wearing diapers and learn how to use the toilet?"

"Yes!" Anders said.

"Awesome!" Mama said. "Should we start tomorrow or right now?"

"Right now!" Anders said.

"Okay," Mama said. "Let's take your diaper off." Anders pulled his pants down and took his diaper off. "When you are naked outside, you can't just start pooping. You must squat down first. If you are wearing clothes, it's the same thing, but you are inside, so you can't just squat down and start pooping! You must run to the toilet instead. The same with pee."

"Okay," Anders said.

They went to the kitchen to have lunch. Today Mama was having sourdough toast topped with kefir cream cheese, wild lox, sliced cucumber, tomato, and red onion, drizzled with olive oil and sprinkled with black pepper. This was one of her favorite meals.

Usually, Anders only ate the lox, which was enough to make this one of his favorite meals too. But today, he took an onion off the top of Mama's tartine and held it up.

"What's that?" he asked.

"Spanish onion or red onion," Mama said.

"Taste it?" Anders asked.

"If you want to," Mama said. Anders took a tiny bite of the onion and made a disgusted face.

"Don't like it!" Anders said.

"I see that! Your face went like this," Mama made a disgusted face so Anders could see. Anders giggled. Anders put the piece of onion back on Mama's plate.

Mama continued chomping away on her tartine while Anders watched her. Then he reached forward and took a piece of onion again. He put the whole big piece in his mouth.

"Mmmmm, that's gooooood. I like that. Yuuuummy!" Anders said, chewing and swallowing.

"Huh," Mama said. "I guess your tastes have changed. Your tastes will change a lot throughout your life. The only important thing is that you pay attention and listen to your body. Speaking of which . . . look at your pants."

Anders looked at his pants. There was a wet spot in the front.

"I think you forgot you are not wearing a diaper," Mama said.

"Ooooooh," Anders said. "I forgot!"

"Yeah," Mama said. "It happens. Let's go get you some new pants."

That day Anders peed in his pants two more times, and then he didn't forget again for the rest of the day. The next day Anders peed in his pants three times and then didn't forget for the rest of the day. The day after that he peed in his pants only one time and then remembered. And on the fourth day he had it all figured out. He never pooped in his pants even once.

He did continue to need diapers while traveling for a year or two, though. It would also be a year or two before Anders had mastered butt wiping and not peeing on the seat.

"I didn't realize what a luxury it was to be squeamish when I was young," Mama said. "Parents can't be squeamish. Parenting is just endless poop. And pee. And vomit. And snot…"

14. The Gym

When Mama was twenty-one years old, she tore a ligament in her knee. When she was twenty-five years old, she developed pain in that knee and went to see a doctor about it. He took an x-ray. He told her that she had arthritis in her knee, that she should take a pain killer whenever her knee hurt, and that when the pain got too bad, she should get knee surgery. He also told her she should never run again.

The order not to run didn't make sense to Mama. If a wild animal hurt its knee and could never run again, it was basically a dead animal. How could the human species have survived if a knee injury was a death sentence? Knee surgery didn't exist for most of human history. And neither did pain killers.

Mama was also worried about the side effects involved in taking pain killers. There were no pills that came without side effects. Even the most innocuous-seeming pain killers like Tylenol listed the side effects of nausea and vomiting as "very common" and stomach pain, diarrhea, constipation, and an enlarged abdomen as "common." Mama wasn't interested in hurting other parts of her body just to hide pain from herself. In fact, she didn't like the idea of hiding pain from herself in the first place.

After talking to many people and doing some research, Mama learned about a way to fix her knee called *physical therapy*.

Mama spent five years doing physical therapy on and off before Anders was born. She had to rework her entire body. When the problem in her knee got better, a new problem showed up in her shoulder; when that got better, a new problem showed up in her hip. It was a long process, but now, as long as Mama did her physical therapy exercises every day, she lived her life free of pain. She could even run about half a mile without any negative consequences.

A few times Mama had gotten busy and stopped doing her exercises. Then, the pain came right back, so Mama learned never to skip her exercises.

When Anders was two, a new gym opened nearby. It was large and quite beautiful. It had a room filled with exercise machines like treadmills, ellipticals, and stationary bicycles. Every machine had its own television. It had a large empty room with soft padding on the floor and mirrors on every wall. The empty room had exercise equipment along one wall like yoga balls, balance pads, and dumbbells. The gym had several large classrooms with wooden floors where instructors taught yoga, pilates, and dance classes. It had a large women's locker room with a spacious vanity where women could blow dry their hair and put on their makeup. The locker room also had bathrooms, showers, a hot tub, and even a sauna. The gym had a men's locker room too, but Mama never saw it. It was most likely pretty similar to the women's locker room. The gym also had a café that sold a variety of coffees, salads, and juices. It was a luxurious gym, and Mama was excited to try it out. She thought it would be nice to get out of the house and do her physical therapy exercises at the gym. She looked forward to taking some of the dance classes as well.

Today was the first day Mama planned to go to the gym. A babysitter Anders liked, named Maria, came over to be with Anders while Mama was gone.

"Bye, Anders. I'm going to the gym," Mama said.

Anders ran to Mama and hugged her legs. "Nooooo!" Anders said.

Mama knelt down to look him in the eye and explained, "I have to go, honey. If I don't go and do my exercises, my back will hurt. Then I will be in pain, and I will be a grouchy Mama. Can you stay and play with Maria for just a little while? I won't be gone long."

"Okay," Anders said. He gave her a big hug and went to find something to do.

The next day when Mama was ready to go, she again said, "Bye, Anders, I'm going to the gym."

He again ran up to her, but this time he did not hug her legs. He looked at her and said, "I come too?"

"I can't bring you with me honey, I'm sorry. My gym doesn't allow kids," she said.

Anders ignored what his mother said and walked confidently to the front door.

"I come too! My back hurts!" he said loudly and with great authority.

Mama, of course, cracked up. Then she said, "Okay, you can come, with Maria, but it will be boring for you. They probably won't let you inside, and you will have to play for an hour in the car while you wait for me."

This was fine with Anders, so they all went to the gym. Mama parked the car in a parking garage.

She, Anders, and Maria entered the gym through a large glass door. Just inside was a counter with a fit young woman in workout clothes standing behind it. Mama handed the woman a card and the woman scanned it into her computer.

"Welcome back, Ms. Ross," she said. "And who is this?" She was referring to Anders who stood nearby, staring at her.

"This is my son, Anders, and his babysitter, Maria," Mama explained. "Anders really wanted to go with me to the gym. I told him there were no children allowed, but he wanted to come and make sure."

The young woman smiled kindly at Anders. "Children are not allowed in here," she said apologetically. "I'm so sorry. When you are sixteen, you may come and work out with your mom."

Mama again knelt down to talk to Anders. "I'm going to go and do my exercises now. I will be out soon. You and Maria will play in the car?"

"Okay, Mama," Anders said. But when Mama started to walk away, Anders tried to go with her. Mama stopped him.

"I can't let you come with me," Mama said. "Children are not allowed in this gym. But you know what, I bet that Maria would let you carry the keys to the car." Anders finally understood. He turned and ran back to Maria. She gave him the keys and they walked to the car. They played there until Mama came out an hour later.

The next three or so times Mama went to the gym, Anders opted to go with her (with his babysitter) and wait in the car until she was done. Then he had had enough of that and decided he would rather stay home while she went to the gym.

A few months later the gym announced that it would provide childcare to children whose parents were using the facilities. Mama toured the childcare room. It had a cartoon movie playing on a large television. Mama asked if it were possible to turn the television off when her child visited as she did not want to expose him to cartoon movies until he was older. The gym representative with whom Mama spoke said that the gym could not do that, as watching movies was the main thing children did there. Mama decided the gym's childcare was not something she would use.

15. Playdate with Truman

Anders was outside playing in the backyard. Papa had made a sandbox, and Anders was sitting in the center of it, talking to himself.

He said, "This my hammer. This my drill gun. These little tools. This little tool. Papa bought this pipe. Bury this pipe. Papa goes outside buried it. We'll need shovels. Papa need shovel. I need shovel. Shovel things. Shovel leaves. Shovel leaves. Shovel leaves! Shovelllleaves! Shovel leeeeeeaves. Shovvvvvvel leavvvvvvves. Shvlvs! Hmmmmm. Both need shovels. I get tired of wind. So much wind! Freezing! Ha ha ha. Mama say that. Freezing! It's freezing! That's my headlamp. That's all my tools. Then I need carry this. Carry this drill gun. Carry this work. Papa need drill gun. Soooo heavy. I'm gunna work on Papa's room. Then Papa comes home. Then I gonna help Papa. I be right back. Then I come right here. Then I help a little bit."

Mama came outside then with Anders's friend, Truman, and said, "Anders, Truman is here to play with you." Truman's mom had just dropped him off.

She was going to go to the grocery store while Truman played with Anders. Anders was happy. He liked Truman. Truman had just turned two, and Anders was two-and-a-half, so they were quite close in age.

Truman immediately joined Anders in the sandbox.

Anders was playing with his toy backhoe. Truman began playing nearby with Anders's front loader. Anders held out his backhoe for Truman to take and said, "Truman! Truck!"

Truman stopped what he was doing and took the backhoe.

"Thanks, Anders! You welcome," he said, knowing that one of those was appropriate to say in this moment, but not really sure which one.

"Welcome! *I* say welcome," Anders said wisely.

Truman pointed to the backhoe, "That *backhoe*," he said. Anders had called it a truck, but it had a more specific name.

"Backhoe," Anders said, nodding. He knew.

"Backhoe," Truman said. Anders pointed at the dump truck at his feet.

"Dump truck," he said.

"Dump truck," Truman agreed.

Anders pointed to its tires, "Has these tires. Drive outside. Turns."

Truman pointed. "This the engine."

Anders pointed. "This the dumper."

Anders was done talking now, so he got between Truman and the dump truck.

"Doing my work," he said. "Don't want play with my toys."

Truman understood and took a few steps away from the dump truck. Then he picked up the backhoe and began to play with it. Anders played with the dump truck. This went on for quite some time, until Truman hurt his thumb.

"Ow!" he said. He ran to Mama who was nearby. He held out his thumb. "Kiss!" he said.

Anders stopped what he was doing, ran to Mama, and dove onto her lap.

"No! That's *my* mom!" Anders said, putting his arms around Mama.

"I am your mom," Mama said to Anders, stroking his head, "but Truman has a hurt thumb, and he wants a kiss." Then she had an idea, "How about you kiss his thumb instead of me?"

Anders shook his head; he didn't want to kiss Truman's thumb. Mama tried another idea, "How about I kiss Truman's thumb, but I stay *your* mom?"

Anders liked this idea and nodded. Mama kissed Truman's thumb, and Truman went back to playing with the backhoe. Anders returned to the dump truck.

An hour or so later Anders and Truman were inside having a snack of raisins and sprouted pine nuts. Anders finished eating and got up from the table. He wanted to knock one of the plastic dining room chairs over to see what would happen. But when he leaned the chair back on its legs, it looked like it would hit Truman if he let go.

Anders said to Truman, "I want knock chair over. Need Truman move."

Truman was munching away on the raisins and pine nuts and didn't notice that Anders had spoken, so Anders said, louder, "I want knock chair over. Need Truman move!"

Again, Truman did not appear to notice. Anders watched him for a bit, his head cocked to the side. Mama sat down in the chair next to Anders. Anders turned to Mama.

"Frustrated," he said.

"Yeah," Mama said. "You want Truman to move, but he didn't hear you. You've been waiting a long time."

Mama turned to Truman and said, "I would normally stop Anders if he wanted to do something as inappropriate as knock a chair over, but yesterday he was in this exact chair and tipped it back too far, and it fell over. It was scary. I think that's why Anders wants to study the chair falling over, and that's why I think it is okay for him to knock it over too, just this once."

Truman looked up from his bowl of raisins and nuts.

"You have Truman's attention now," Mama said to Anders, "Do you want to tell him again what you want?"

But Anders didn't have to say anything because Truman had understood. He climbed down from his chair and stood a few feet from the table.

"Thank, Truman!" Anders said.

Anders knocked his chair over and giggled with glee. Truman wasn't sure whether he felt delighted or concerned, but he was interested in what Anders had done and watched him closely.

"Never tip a chair back when you are sitting in it," Mama said. "See how easy it falls over. Ouch."

"Ouch," Truman agreed.

"Ouch," Anders agreed as well.

Anders tried to stand the chair back up on his own, but he was not able to, so Mama helped. And that was it. Anders was done with his experiment, and Truman returned to eating.

16. Renaissance Fair

One day in May, Anders found a small piece of paper with writing on it. He said to himself, "What this? This a list! Shopping list. Home Depot. I need go Home Depot. Got a list. I go Home Depot. I get dressed up. I need go Home Depot get real bulldozer, real excavator. I got get keys. I go way, way, way far. I go Home Depot be right back. Then I get home, I see Mama, hangout playroom, then we build train track. Go Home Depot buy stuff. Need list. Need keys...."

Anders played this game again and again, pretending to find the list and then planning out what it was for. When he was done, he went to find Mama.

"Mama love Papa?" he asked.

"Yeah, Mama love Papa," Mama replied.

"Iiiiiiiiiiii love Papa too," he said. "Papa super cute. Super fancy."

Mama smiled. Papa wore suits to work every day, and he did look elegant in them.

"I think so too," Mama said. "Speaking of fancy, would you like to go to the Renaissance Fair with me today? You will see some fancy people there."

Anders had no idea what a Renaissance Fair was, but he was generally enthusiastic to go everywhere, especially if it sounded like a new adventure. So, with his customary big smile and nodding head, he said, "Yes!"

They drove an hour to the Hoover Dam Recreation Area where the Renaissance Fair was held every year. Mama parked the car in a giant dirt parking lot as close to the entrance of the fair as she could. As soon as Anders got out of the car, he knew he was about to go somewhere special.

Everywhere Anders looked there were people who had either just arrived like him and were headed towards the fair or there were people who had been at the fair all day and were headed home. Many looked like people he might see at the park any day, but many others looked nothing like people he had ever seen before. There were women wearing giant dresses with skirts as wide as a doorway, and there were men wearing hats and carrying swords. As they walked toward the entrance of the fair Anders saw a man on stilts whose legs seemed to be longer than Mama was tall.

Soon Anders and Mama stood in front of a large wall. On the right, people leaving the fair streamed out and on the left, people entering the fair handed tickets to a man standing guard. Mama gave the tickets to Anders.

"Would you like to hand the man the tickets?" Mama asked.

Anders took them, wordlessly, entranced by his surroundings. He handed them to the man standing guard at the entrance.

"Welcome!" the guard said. "What a little gentleman! Paying for the lady, are you?"

Anders smiled at him, but he said nothing. Mama thought he might not know what to say, so she said, "You can say, 'Yes, I am, Sir.'"

"Yes, I am, Sir," Anders said to the man.

"What a gentleman!" the man said again. "What a lucky lady to have such a boy!"

Mama smiled, and she and Anders continued forward into the fair.

The fair was designed to look like a thriving town during the time of the Renaissance. It had a wide, main street down which people could walk. There were interesting attractions on both sides of the road. There were booths that sold artisanal crafts like jewelry, soaps, perfumes, and home decorating items. There were many small shops that sold shoes and clothing, most of which was from the Renaissance period. There were shops that sold armor and swords and other interesting weapons, and shops that sold metal crowns with jewels on them. There were booths that sold food and ale. There were also rides and games—there was a giant swing, and a maze people could walk through.

The first attraction at which Anders wanted to stop was a tent where women were using spinning wheels to spin wool into yarn. Anders watched the women work for a long time. Eventually he reached his arms out. He wanted to try it too, but the women said, "No," so he and Mama moved on.

At another tent, strong-looking men worked with metal. They heated pieces of metal in a hot fire and then, when the metal was red hot, they took it out and pounded on it with hammers. Sparks flew while the metal slowly accepted the shape it was being hammered into. Anders thought this was even more interesting than the last tent. He watched the men for so long that Mama ended up getting out her book and reading while she waited for Anders to have his fill.

When Anders was finally done watching the blacksmiths, he and Mama stopped by a booth where a man sold wreaths of flowers for people to wear on their heads. Mama bought a pink one for herself and a blue one for Anders.

Then Mama asked, "What do you want to do next? Do you want to get something to eat or go see the animals?"

"The animals!" Anders said.

They walked to the petting zoo. It was far. They got so tired of walking that they almost decided to skip the petting zoo, but they ended up making it there. Anders got to see rabbits, chickens, pigs, sheep, goats, and miniature horses.

The miniature horses were his favorite. He spent quite a bit of time gathering little pieces of hay from the ground and putting it through the fence into the horses' stalls.

When Anders was done with the animals, Mama bought some meat pies, and she and Anders sat down on hay bales to eat. The hay bales were set up in long rows, like benches. They surrounded a stage no one was performing on at the moment.

"This so good!" Anders said, eating his meat pie.

"Right?" Mama said. "I love meat pies!"

Suddenly, a group of three kids around ten years old, laughing and shouting, started running down the rows of hay bales. They had swords in their hands and ran down one row and then jumped from that row to the next row. Then they ran up the new row to its end and jumped to the next row.

Anders loved their game and decided to try it out for himself. He stood up and ran down the row of hay bales where he had been sitting. He knew that he was not big enough to jump from that row to the next, so he climbed down, walked two steps to the next row of hay bales, and then climbed up. Then, following the path of the big kids, he ran up that row of hay bales, climbed down at the end, took two steps to the next row, and climbed up.

This went on for quite some time. Mama got lots of reading done. Now it was getting late, so they started heading for the exit, but they had a long way to go. When they were about halfway back, Mama stopped at a small shop that mixed scented oils into perfumes. She and Anders took a break from walking and smelled lots of interesting things. Then Mama ordered a perfume to be made of three different scents mixed together.

"The ones in the stores have so many chemicals in them" she explained to Anders. "I love the idea of buying pure oils mixed together—no chemicals." Anders smiled. He looked tired. "What do you think of the Renaissance Fair?" Mama asked.

"I love it," said Anders.

"Me too," said Mama. "I love the beautiful little walking streets and the people everywhere in their beautiful costumes. I love a town centered around not driving. And didn't you think everyone was super friendly and nice?"

"Yeah," said Anders.

The sun was setting now, and a parade started. At the front, bagpipers and drummers played music. Behind them people danced. Anders joined in, following the dancers, and mimicking them. The dancers saw him and invited him to dance with them. He joined them for a while, but soon he was too tired to continue and sat down on the side of the little dirt street for a rest.

"Can't walk anymore," he said. "Carry me?"

"I can't carry you," Mama said. "But when you are done resting, how about we play tag?"

"Okay," said Anders.

When he was done resting, Mama said, "I'm going to get you!" Anders laughed happily and began to run. Mama chased him, saying, "I'm going to get you!" every now and then. When Anders got tired Mama said, "Okay, now you're it, and you try to get me!" Anders perked up and started chasing Mama. "Don't get me!" she called, looking behind her every few seconds to make sure Anders was still following her. Soon they had made it to the car.

When Anders finally got into his car seat, he fell asleep before Mama had even started the car.

17. The Airport Again

"Is everyone ready to go?" Papa asked.

Mama and Anders said they were, so Papa used an app on his phone to call an Uber, a car that would drive them to the airport.

They were headed back to the farm in Nicaragua. They wanted to make the farm nicer. Papa was going to build a water system. He would need to move water from the dam he had built in the creek to the kitchen and bathroom. Then they would have running water. Next, he needed to install a hot water heater, so that they would have hot water. Finally, he planned to develop a pump and gravity system so that they would have good water pressure. Papa had been studying water systems for the last few months and was looking forward to putting into practice what he had learned.

"You never think about how hard it is to move water from one place to another and get it to behave how you want it to," Papa said. "All my life I have just turned on a faucet if I wanted water. I never thought about how complicated it was to get the water to come through that faucet."

Mama agreed. "Taking raw land and turning it into a comfortable life is . . . a daunting task."

While Papa worked on the water system, Mama and Anders were going to work on the rooms. The rooms needed to be more comfortable, more efficient, and more pleasing to look at. They needed real mattresses, cotton sheets, new pillows, glass windows, curtains, curtain rods, a desk and a chair, a place to put clothes away, and a shelf for books and games. The rooms also needed air-conditioning, dehumidifying, and bug-proofing.

Accomplishing these goals would not be easy because one could not purchase everything in Nicaragua that one could purchase in the United States. Therefore Papa, Mama, and Anders were bringing a lot of stuff with them to the farm. They had packed twelve pieces of luggage, the maximum their airline would allow. They had six huge bags to be checked, each weighing fifty pounds, and five of their six carry-ons were packed with as much as carry-on bags could hold—which also turned out to be about fifty pounds, if they were packed carefully. Only one carry-on didn't weigh fifty pounds and that was

Anders's carry-on, a small rolling suitcase, which he packed himself, filled with his favorite toys.

The Uber arrived. It was not easy to fit all the luggage—and three people—into the car, but finally they did it, and they were able to head to the airport. The drive to the airport took an hour. Then it was time to move the twelve pieces of luggage from the car to the check-in line.

Mama stood at the back of the long line. Papa brought bag after bag to her from the car. Anders went back and forth with Papa, helping him by pushing on the bags while Papa pulled. When all twelve bags were there, Papa and Anders joined Mama in line.

The line was long, and it moved slowly. Every time the line moved, they had to move all twelve bags. There was hardly any downtime because every time they had finally finished moving all twelve bags to their new place in line, the line would move again, and they would need to start moving the twelve bags all over again. It was exhausting work. Papa was relieved when they finally reached the check-in counter.

At the check-in counter, Papa gave the airline representative the family's passports, and she typed away at her computer screen for a few minutes. She printed tickets and handed them to Papa. Then she had

Papa place each suitcase on a scale, so that she could verify its weight. None of the suitcases weighed over fifty pounds, so she put luggage tags on them and heaved them onto a moving conveyer belt behind her. The luggage would travel down the conveyer belt to the airport's luggage room where it would be sorted into waiting baggage carts. The baggage carts designated for their plane would then be driven by an airport employee to their plane where the suitcases would finally be loaded on.

Papa thanked the airline representative. Anders began rolling his suitcase. Papa picked up the five remaining bags. He put one backpack on his back and one on his front; he hung a duffle bag from his shoulder and then picked up the two remaining duffle bags, one in each hand.

Papa was carrying a total of two hundred and fifty pounds. Despite repeated offers, he wouldn't let Mama carry any of the bags, partly because her old injury made it risky for her to carry anything and partly because Papa believed it was good manners for men to carry things, as men are much stronger than women.

"I cannot believe what you are doing right now," Mama said. "Do you need a break? You look like you are suffering so much!"

"I am suffering," Papa said. "But I know we will look back on this time in our lives and laugh."

The family left the check-in counter and made their way to the security line. Again, the line was long. Papa put down the five bags he was carrying. Anders added his little rolling suitcase to the pile. This time it was easy to keep up with the line because moving six bags every time the line moved didn't take long.

Once they reached the front of the line and were at the security checkpoint, they had to remove all the electronics from their carry-on bags and place them in special trays. They also had to remove their shoes, their sweaters, and anything in their pockets and put those things in special trays. Then the bags and the trays went through an x-ray machine.

Adults were expected to go through an x-ray machine as well, called a body scanner. Children were not expected to expose their young bodies to the radiation of the body scanner, so Anders, with Mama and Papa, were invited to skip the body scanner and walk through a metal detector instead.

Once they were done with security, it was time to walk to their gate. Papa picked up the five, heavy, carry-on bags, and Anders wheeled his little suitcase. LAX is a big airport, and their gate was the last one in the terminal, so the walk was excruciatingly far. At one point Anders got tired of rolling his little bag and asked Mama to carry it for him, but Papa said, "Anders, if I can handle this load, I think you can handle that one." Anders agreed.

Once they were at their gate, Anders unzipped his suitcase, and spread his toys around him. He began playing with his construction trucks. Mama sat nearby reading, and Papa worked on his computer.

"Mama, give me water truck," Anders said, pointing at the fire truck near her. Mama was confused.

"Do you mean the fire truck?"

Anders said, "No, water truck. Carries water. Oh! Carries fire?"

"Anders, you are totally right," Mama said. "It doesn't carry fire; it carries water. Water truck makes perfect sense. It's called a fire truck because it carries water specifically to put out fires. But you can call it a water truck if you want. I will know what you mean. Other people might not though."

Anders decided he would go back to calling that type of truck a fire truck.

18. Airport Food

Three hours later, the family had arrived at the airport in Houston, Texas where they had a layover before their next flight, the one that would take them to Nicaragua. Papa, with the two hundred and fifty pounds of carry-on luggage, went ahead to their next gate. He wanted to get some work done.

Mama and Anders went to acquire dinner. This was tricky because most food sold at airports is highly processed, which Mama and Papa could tolerate but which made Anders vomit. Anders had vomited every time he had eaten airport food so far, so Mama examined every restaurant at the airport before settling on the one she thought served the least junky food.

"Where would you like to sit?" Mama asked once they were inside the restaurant. Anders chose to sit at the bar and climbed up onto the barstool all by himself. Mama ordered mussels for Anders and her to share, but Anders liked them so much that he ate them all! Mama ordered a second plate.

While they were waiting for the second plate of mussels, Anders studied the show on the television above the bar, trying to figure out what the men pictured on the screen were doing.

Though the family did not own a television, Anders was familiar with it as he had seen it at stores, restaurants, and friends' houses. He was also familiar with moving pictures as Mama explained many things to him by showing him videos from the internet. She also took endless videos of him that he enjoyed watching.

"They're having a running party right there!" Anders told Mama, pointing at the screen. Mama glanced at the football game on the TV and smiled. It *did* look like a running party.

Soon it was time for Mama and Anders to go to their gate and meet up with Papa.

"Thank you!" said Papa when Anders handed him his dinner of fish and chips.

"You're welcome," said Anders.

"How did it go?" asked Mama

"I love technology," Papa said, shutting his computer. "I just got so much work done. It's so amazing how, with the internet, we can work pretty much from anywhere. I love going into my office and working with everyone there, but I also love being free to get my work done in other places, like airports on my way to my farm in Nicaragua!"

19. Nicaragua Again

Anders, now two years and eight months old, was happy to be back at the farm. No friends came with the family this time, but there were still many people at the farm. There was Nate, the farm manager who was also Mama's cousin. He was from Montana and had been living at the farm in quite rough conditions for over a year but remained a happy and enthusiastic guy. There was also James, a stylish older man from Idaho who had heard about the farm from Nate's mother and had recently moved there to work as the cook for a few years while learning Spanish. There was also Max and his team of workers who came to the farm six days each week to work on building projects. And, more exciting than the humans, there was Brava, a little puppy Nate and James had recently purchased for ten dollars.

"A farm needs a guard dog," Nate said. "James and I will make Brava a good one."

Anders loved Brava, and for the first week he was at the farm, he carried her everywhere he went.

In the six months since the last time the family had been at the farm, Max and his team had built a new building, a duplex. The duplex was built at an awkward angle to the fourplex, which was built at an awkward angle to the small, one-room building that served as the office.

"Why are the buildings all angled so weird?" Mama asked.

"Nate says its Max's fault, and Max says it's Nate's fault," Papa said. "What I have learned is that it's really risky to have anything built when I am not here in person to oversee it.... Come see the new duplex. The rooms are big enough so that you, Anders, and me can all sleep in the same room."

"Great," said Mama.

"Yay!" said Anders.

Papa pushed open a heavy, rough wooden door that looked glued together. It didn't open easily and made quite a bit of noise when it finally moved.

"I don't know why there's so much space at the bottom," Papa said. The bottom of the door was at least two inches from the floor, and as they were soon to find out, that allowed for an endless parade of bugs and spiders to enter the room.

"You have to be careful when you are turning the light on and off, or you will get shocked," Papa said, showing Mama the electrical switch hanging loosely out of the wall and how if she touched the back, she would get shocked. "You won't die or anything, but it'll hurt."

A single light bulb with no cover hung from the ceiling in the center of the room. It didn't offer much light, but Mama and Anders could see the room well enough. The floors were not dusty cement, as the fourplex rooms had been. They were tiled in a bright orange Spanish tile. The walls were not dusty cement either, as the fourplex walls had been. They were painted an ultra-bright white. The room was sparsely furnished with a rough bunk bed where Anders would sleep and a big bed where Mama and Papa would sleep. There were still no mattresses; all the beds had the same thin, foam cushions as before. Instead of the ill-fitting screens like the fourplex had, this room had ill-fitting plastic windows with no curtains. An inexpensive air conditioner on wheels was hooked up to one of the windows.

"Yay! Air-conditioning!" Mama said. She went straight to the air conditioner and stood right in front of it. "This will really help when I need a break from the heat." The air conditioner was more like a cooling fan than an actual air conditioner, but a cooling fan was better than nothing.

Anders loved the new room. More specifically, he loved the bunk bed. He slept on the bottom bunk but was obsessed with figuring out how to get to the top bunk. It took him a solid week of dedicated hard work to figure out how to climb onto the top bunk, but when he did, that was where he could be found for hours at a time. Then he spent a week figuring out how to get himself and a toy onto the top bunk. Soon the top bunk was a storage place for all of Anders's favorite things: his hammers, his screw drivers, his tape measures, his level, his carpenter's square, and his shovel. One day, Anders even figured out how to get Brava up there.

The rancho, the wooden building with only three sides, now had a kitchen and dining area. There was a picnic table with two benches where people could eat meals. There was a kitchen area comprised of a wood counter with a camping stove and a toaster oven on it, a large fridge with a broken door that had been kindly donated by Papa's friend Ken, and a sink that would soon be able to run cold water. The floor had aged since the last time they were there. Now when they walked on the wood plank floor, the wood planks curved under their weight.

Even so, all were happy that they would no longer need to walk in the hot sun to Lillian's for meals.

The bathroom had changed slightly. Next to the toilet stall there was a rough cement stall with a shower that was hooked up to pipes and could run a trickle of cold water. The toilet stall, however, was the same rough cement stall with the five-gallon bucket under a toilet seat made of rough wood.

"Every time I sit down, I swear I get a splinter in my butt!" Mama said. She had come with printouts of a beautifully made wood cover for a bucket toilet someone made in Australia. The toilet looked like the white porcelain toilets in Los Angeles, just made of wood and with a bucket under the toilet seat instead of plumbing.

Mama gave these pictures to a local woodworker, and in three weeks the toilet was no longer a scary thing to sit on. Not only was the new, wood toilet smooth and comfortable, it was even a little beautiful.

At dinner, the first night after the new toilet was unveiled at the farm, everyone was seated around the picnic table in the rancho eating rice and beans and sharing stories from their day.

Mama said, "As of today, there is finally beauty to gaze at here at the farm … the toilet." Everyone laughed. Then Mama added, "What do you guys think of it?"

"It's the best-looking toilet I've ever seen," said James laughing.

"I didn't have a problem with the old one, and I don't have a problem with the new one," said Nate in his mountain-man way.

"It's literally the most beautiful toilet in the world," Papa said. "And it's even more beautiful because we are composting our nutrients and turning them into valuable soil."

"Yeah," Mama agreed, "I don't love scooping sawdust every time I go to the bathroom, but I absolutely love that we are properly appreciating our poop!"

Nate cracked up. "Appreciating our poop!" he said, laughing.

"'Preciating our poop!" Anders said, laughing too.

"I'm serious!" Mama said. "It's a big deal! Think of it this way: In Los Angeles the big ash tree in our back yard takes nutrients from our soil and uses those nutrients to grow taller and make leaves. Each October the leaves fall, and we rake them up, put them in trash bags, and pay money to have them taken away. Each leaf is made of our soil, the nutrients from our soil. And they get kicked off our land. And then our soil is depleted, so we go and spend money on fertilizer. Sewage is no different—it must be taken care of properly, but the idea is the same. Nutrients are valuable. The leftover nutrients from our food, in the city, get thrown in the trash and flushed down the drain. Those nutrients were expensive! In the city, I can't keep them, but here at our farm, we plan to keep *all* of our nutrients!"

"Here, here!" Nate said holding his beer up for a toast. James, Papa, Mama, and Anders all put their glasses in and clinked them around. "To poop!" Nate said. James and Papa laughed. Mama shook her head. Anders laughed so hard he almost fell off the bench.

Anders thought toasting to poop was so funny that for that night, and many nights afterward, everyone toasted to poop again and again.

20. The Wet Season

It was exciting to be at the farm in July, one of the wettest months of the year in Nicaragua. Once or twice each day, or even three or four times, there was a torrential downpour of rain that lasted for about fifteen minutes. It was magical, and every time it happened Mama and Anders shouted, "Woohoo!" and ran out into the storm to dance around.

Sometimes there was thunder that boomed so loudly it felt like the earth was shaking. Mama told Anders that their ancestors said thunder was caused by a god named Thor when he was fighting frost giants.

"So, whenever we hear thunder, we can say, 'Go, Thor! Get those frost giants!' if we want," Mama said.

"That's silly," Anders said.

"I know," Mama said. "It's not a true story. But it sure is fun to give thunder a name and a personality and make up anthropomorphic stories about it."

Anders agreed, so sometimes when the thunder was exceptionally loud, he would yell, "Go, Thor!"

The locals thought Mama and Anders were nuts. When it rained, they stopped their work and found shelter until the rain passed. They never got wet in the rain on purpose. Mama explained to them that in Los Angeles it only ever rains three or four days out of the entire year, and even then, it rarely rains hard, so rain was special and fun for her and Anders.

The locals still thought they were nuts.

The only bad thing about all the rain was that it meant a major increase in the various bug populations that plagued the farm. The ants seemed to be everywhere. They were especially common in the grass between the duplex and the rancho, where Mama had to walk for every meal and every time she wanted to go to the bathroom. Getting bitten by ants one to two dozen times a day became just a fact of life for Mama. Anders had so many bug bites he always looked like he had the chicken pox.

The little black jungle wasps also seemed to be everywhere now. Every other day there was a new hive that needed to be knocked out of the rancho. Nate, who was tough and brave, was always the person who knocked out the hives, and even though he knocked out a dozen hives over the course of the summer, he was never stung by any of the wasps.

Both Nate and James had been stung by scorpions, though. So had Brava.

"She was just being a curious puppy, and she saw a scorpion and started sniffing it," James told everyone. "And the scorpion stung her. She was so upset! She yelped and whined for a long time. After that she basically declared war on all scorpions and tries to fight and kill any she finds."

"How does she fight and kill them?" Mama asked.

"She snaps at them with her teeth," James said.

Sure enough, one night Mama woke up to go to the bathroom and heard the small dog snarling. Mama shone her headlamp to see what was going on, and there was Brava, fighting it out with a scorpion in the pitch black.

Neither Mama, nor Papa, nor Anders, was stung by a scorpion that summer, even though there were many opportunities. Once, when Mama was putting Anders to bed, she pulled back the sheet, and there was a huge scorpion, right there where Anders was just about to lie down.

Because the rooms had no furniture besides beds, they lived out of their suitcases on the floor. That was where Mama found a scorpion every day for the first week of their visit. Then she learned to always keep her suitcase zipped closed. She didn't find scorpions as often after that.

Many of the bugs didn't bother Mama and Anders at all, like the whip spider that lived in the shower. Whip spiders are huge spiders that look like small, thin, lobsters. They have broad, flat, black bodies about two inches across and long legs that stretch out to six inches or so.

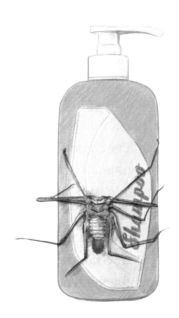

At first, Mama and Anders found whip spiders terrifying, but then they learned that whip spiders don't sting or bite. If you mess with them, they can cut you, but they don't want to; they are shy spiders by nature and will leave you alone if you leave them alone.

"What that?!" Anders asked one night as they were finishing their dinner in the rancho.

Beyond the rancho, it was dark as usual but there were a dozen or so bright, little lights hovering a few feet off the ground. They looked like fairies.

"Are those fireflies?!" Mama cried.

"Yeah," Nate said. "This is firefly season. If we turn off all the lights, even more will come out."

"Let's do it!" Anders said. Nate turned out the lights, and the courtyard became dark in a way that only a farm, miles from other lights, with no city on the horizon, can be. Each minute more and more fireflies came out. Anders climbed onto Mama's lap and Papa put his arm around them. It wasn't long before the courtyard was a dazzling show. The small lights hovered above the ground and flashed on and off. It looked like they were dancing.

"This is called entertainment at the farm," said James. "No TV, nope, for fun we sit around and watch the bugs."

"But it's such a satisfying activity!" Mama said. "This is magical."

They watched the fireflies for a long time and then headed to the bathroom to brush their teeth.

"Is frog there?" asked Anders.

"Yes, he is," Mama said, lifting Anders up so he could see their sink friend, the little, green frog that lived in the bathroom sink.

"Sooooo cute!" Anders said.

Anders became quite attached to the little green frog that summer and for years afterward would comment that bathrooms without little, green sink frogs were lonely, boring places.

21. Decorating Trip to Managua

Now Papa was back in Los Angeles, working. He had succeeded in bringing the rancho and the bathroom running water, but there was little water pressure and no hot water yet.

While Papa was gone, Mama and Anders set about decorating the duplex rooms. This meant endless trips to Managua. Mama learned that Sunday was the best day to drive in Nicaragua, as there was less traffic on the road. They started driving to Managua every Friday. It took four hours. When they drove back on Sunday, it took only three hours.

Mama and Anders enjoyed the breaks from life at the farm. Life at the farm was like camping at a construction site. Mama loved camping, but not for longer than a week. Living in such rough conditions for three months, with such intense sun and heat exposure and the endless bug bites was draining. Mama loved how peaceful life was at the farm without the internet, but she also appreciated being able to use the internet when she was in the city. She also enjoyed bathing in hot water.

On each trip to Managua, Mama and Anders did reconnaissance on Spanish-style decorating by staying at different hotels around the city and taking pictures of doors, windows, floors, and furniture they liked. This made each trip to Managua a different adventure.

Today was Saturday and Ken had generously loaned Mama his assistant, Alex for the day. Alex was going to chauffer Mama and Anders to various stores around the city so they could buy things for the farm.

"Where do you want to go first?" Alex asked.

"Sinsa," said Mama.

"Sinsa!" said Anders, jumping up and down in excitement.

Alex laughed.

"Sinsa is like Disneyland for Anders, I think," he said.

"I think you are right," Mama agreed.

Sinsa was the largest hardware and home improvement chain store in Nicaragua. It was similar to Home Depot and sold many of the same brands.

When they got to Sinsa, Anders completely ignored the children's play area set up in the front of the store and instead got a little basket with wheels on the bottom and a long handle that he could pull behind him. He walked down aisle after aisle looking at things. Whenever he found something that he wanted to buy, he put it into his basket. Alex stayed with him, so that Mama could focus on color schemes for the bedrooms.

Mama got a few dozen paint color cards, a dozen wood tint color cards, and doorknobs in brass, stainless steel, and imitation iron. Then she sat at a table in the café area and got out a piece of the orange tile used for the floor that she kept in her purse. She put the floor tile in the middle of the table and made different combinations for the walls, furniture, and hardware around it. Anders and Alex stopped by.

"Which of these sets looks best with the floor tile?" Mama asked Anders.

"That one," said Anders, instantly, pointing to a pale gray paint card sitting with an espresso-colored wood tint card and a doorknob made if imitation iron.

"Yes, that one looks quite nice," Mama said. Anders and Alex went back to exploring the store and Mama continued to try out different color combinations.

Thirty minutes later Mama settled on what Anders had liked: a pale gray color for the walls to tone down and complement the orange tile, an espresso-colored wood tint for the furniture she was having made for the room, and a dark, imitation iron doorknob.

After Mama placed her order with the paint technician, she went about collecting other things the room needed: she found black, imitation iron curtain rods, lamps, door handles, hat hooks, and a mirror.

After they had been at Sinsa for three hours, it was finally time to check out. Mama told Anders to go through his basket and choose one item, the thing he wanted the most, and she would buy it for him. Anders chose a hammer.

"But you already have a hammer," said Mama.

"Need *this* hammer," said Anders.

"Okay," said Mama laughing. "While I am buying these things, I want you to go around with Alex and put the rest of the things in your basket back."

"Okay," said Anders.

Checking out took an hour, so by the time they were leaving, they had been at Sinsa for four hours.

"I am bleary-eyed and starving!" Mama said.

"Me too!" Anders said.

Right across the highway from Sinsa was a restaurant called Ola Verde, where Mama and Anders liked to eat. Ola Verde was the only restaurant in

Managua that served organic food. It was owned by an American expat named Carla.

At Ola Verde, as at every other restaurant Mama and Anders had been to in Nicaragua, it took ten minutes to get a menu, twenty minutes to get a glass of water, and at least forty-five minutes to get a meal. Mama ordered the same soup and salad that she always ordered, and Anders ordered the same curry and rice that he always ordered. The food was delicious.

After eating, Alex took Mama and Anders to a strip mall with over two dozen fabric stores. The mall had a carousel where Alex took Anders while Mama went into the nearest fabric store to find linen.

The store was small and dark. It did not have air-conditioning, so it was overwhelmingly hot and humid. Mama perused the fabrics. After ten minutes of searching, she had found nothing but polyester, so she approached the salesclerk.

"Excuse me," Mama said in Spanish. "Do you have any linen fabric?"

"What?" the clerk said.

"I am looking for linen fabric," Mama said.

The salesclerk shook her head. "I have never heard of that," the clerk said. Mama took a piece of paper out of her purse and wrote the word *lino* on it. The salesclerk looked at the paper and continued to shake her head and say she had never heard of it.

"Do you have any cotton?" Mama asked.

"No," the woman said. "No one sells cotton here. But I have things that look like cotton." The woman motioned for Mama to follow her, and she got out a few rolls of fabric that did not look at all like cotton to Mama.

"Thank you," Mama said. She smiled and left the store. She went into the store next door and asked the salesclerk if she had any linen or cotton fabric. The woman said neither of those fabrics were sold in Nicaragua and then tried to interest Mama in polyester fabrics that she thought resembled them. Mama again did not think the polyester fabrics resembled linen at all, so she thanked the clerk and left the store.

The same thing happened at the next three stores. Mama could not tell if the salesclerks were being honest — that there really wasn't any linen available for sale in the country — or if they were lying to her in the hopes that she would buy an imitation linen from them.

Luckily, at the sixth store Mama went into a kind salesclerk pointed to a fabric store in the middle of the strip mall and told Mama that that one sold expensive fabrics like linen. Mama thanked the woman profusely and went to the store at which she had pointed. Unfortunately, the store only had three linen fabrics for sale, and none were white. The salesclerk at that store told Mama that no other store in the shopping center sold linen. Mama thanked her, returned to the store with the kind salesclerk, and gave her $5[6] for her honesty. Her name was Ana, and Mama wrote down both her name and the store at which she worked so that Mama would know where to go the next time she needed to buy fabric.

In the meantime, Mama asked Ana if there were any other stores that sold linen. Ana asked the person at the store next door to watch her store for a minute, and then she proceeded to walk Mama to the other two stores at the strip mall that sold linen. Ana spoke for Mama when they went into the two stores, explaining to the salesclerks what Mama was looking for. Soon Mama had linen samples in white, off-white, cream, and yellow. Mama thanked Ana again and gave her a second $5 tip for her help.

---

[6] Five dollars is a huge tip in Nicaragua. Nicaraguan salesclerks make around $5 for an entire day's labor.

Now Mama and Anders were super tired, but there was still one more store on their list: Siman. Siman was an elegant department store. There, Anders perused the toy section with Alex while Mama bought a doormat, towels, a set of sheets, a trash bin, and a set of gray and white patio furniture. Mama thought she and Anders were finally done for the day, but when she checked out, she was told that the patio furniture was not in the store, and that they would need to drive to a warehouse about thirty minutes away to pick it up.

When they were finally done for the day and back at the hotel, Anders put on his swimming clothes and played on the steps of the pool, while Mama rested in a chair nearby.

Back at the farm, Mama spent a long time with the fabric samples trying to decide which hue looked best in the space. Anders thought the whitest one looked the best. Mama eventually agreed.

"Anders, you have such a good eye for beauty! And you're so fast!" Mama said admiringly.

Now it was time for Mama to figure out how to get a nicer door. The problem was that when Mama had asked Max to make a nicer door for their room, he appeared to think that the current door was perfect, and there was nothing wrong with it.

When Mama was in Managua, she had spent some time on the internet researching Spanish-style doors and had saved a picture of a door she liked. Max said there was no way he could make a door like that, but he knew a guy who could. So, he drove Mama to a workshop in Acoyapa owned by a man named Carlos. Carlos said he could make the door, and he did.

But though the door looked like the one in the picture, it didn't look well-made. Mama could not figure out why. Mama was having other issues with Angel in Juigalpa, who had made several items of furniture for the room. All the furniture he made for Mama did look well made, it just was never what she had designed. Mama couldn't drive an hour and a half every day to check on the furniture she had ordered to make sure it was being made as she specified. She decided that she needed a furniture maker to work at the farm, so that she could check on the work each day and catch mistakes.

Carlos recommended a man named Erick. When Mama met Erick, she liked him immediately. Unlike Max, Carlos, Lillian, Trinio and all the other people Mama had met so far, Erick slowed down his speech and annunciated when he spoke with her.

Mama found him easier to communicate with than anyone else she had met.

Erick began coming to the farm each day to tint, sand, and build anything made of wood that Mama wanted for the rooms. It took Mama many tries to get Erick to understand that she didn't need him to be fast, she only wanted high-quality work. But eventually, he understood, and the woodwork at the farm ended up being strikingly beautiful.

When Papa came back to the farm in August, he couldn't believe his eyes. The rough, ugly room he had left, now looked comfortable.

"It feels nice to be in here," Papa said. "I honestly don't even know what you did, but it feels really good."

"You know what I did!" Mama said, and then she went over every detail with him: the star lights hanging out front that had come in a suitcase with Papa; the door that was designed to complement the lights; the door hinges and handle whose colors matched the color of the wood tint; the subtle gray color of the walls; the bright color of the ceiling; the molding around the floor and the ceiling; the molding around the windows; the dark-colored entry table, desk, chair, wardrobe, and bedside tables.

"I can appreciate so much what you have done," Papa said, "but I could never have done it."
Mama felt proud.

22. Selva Negra

Now Papa was back in Los Angeles, and Dave, a family friend who was curious about Papa's project in Nicaragua, came to visit.

After Dave spent a week on the farm in perfect tranquility, Mama asked him and Anders if they wanted to go on a reconnaissance adventure.

"Ken just visited a hotel with a farm. It's called Selva Negra, and it's four hours north of here. He says we absolutely must see it. Want to go?" she asked.

"Yes!" said Anders.

"Sure," said Dave.

Selva Negra was in the mountains. Getting there was a little scary because the mountain highway was narrow, winding, steep, and had no guard rails.

"Get too far out of your lane and off the side of the mountain you go," Mama said, holding Anders close as Dave drove.

Eventually they turned off the highway onto a dirt road. At a guard tower, they gave their names and entered the resort.

Selva Negra was built in the late 1800s by a group of German immigrants from an area of Germany called Bavaria. It had a dining hall overlooking a large pond and little cabins sprinkled throughout the forest. The dining hall and cabins were cute. They were painted red and green and looked like they had been transplanted straight from Bavaria.

Surrounding the cabins and the dining hall was old-growth rainforest. The trees were wide and extremely tall, and they shaded the whole area. There was no direct sunlight on the property. When Mama, Anders, and Dave got out of the car, they were surprised to find that the temperature was quite cold.

"I have never been cold in Nicaragua before. I didn't know there were cold areas of this country!" Mama said.

"The name is appropriate," said Dave. "Selva Negra—black forest. I can't believe how dark it is in here."

A bellman showed Mama and Anders to their little cabin in the woods. Another bellman showed Dave to his. After they had unpacked, Mama and Anders met up with Dave to go for a walk through the forest. They stopped many times to admire various trees. Mama was sad that Papa had already bought their farm. This area was so beautiful, and the weather was so much more bearable. If they had only known before, they could have bought a farm in the mountains.

After their walk, Mama, Anders, and Dave went to the dining hall for dinner. Mama ordered a German dish called schnitzel, and Anders ordered the cheese plate. Selva Negra had its own cheese maker, who made a variety of European cheeses, like Manchego, Gouda, and Swiss.

Dave, Mama, and Anders were the only guests at the resort, besides an American couple at a table near them. Even though the restaurant was almost empty, it took almost an hour for their meal to arrive.

"I'm pretty sure you order your meal, and then they go to the store to buy the ingredients," Mama heard the woman joke to her husband.

Anders didn't eat much of his dinner, so he asked for a to-go box. That way he would have a snack for later in case he got hungry.

After dinner it was so dark that it was hard for Mama and Anders to find their little cabin, but they found it eventually and went straight to bed. They were tired.

In the middle of the night, a strange noise woke Mama up. It sounded creepy. Mama had no idea what kind of animal it could be, but it sounded angry, loud, threatening, and vaguely human. It also sounded like it was right outside their secluded little cabin and wanted in.

Mama felt afraid. It sounded like there were animals on the roof and some were pulling at the wooden shutters on the windows. Mama got out of bed and made sure all the shutters were closed tight and the door was locked. The noise went on for quite some time; Mama shivered in bed and cuddled up close to Anders, who was sleeping peacefully despite the nightmarish racket.

Mama practiced mimicking the sound with her mouth so she could describe it to Anders the next day. She sucked air into her mouth with her mouth open and allowed the air to vibrate against her throat, making a gasping-for-air kind of noise, then she widened her mouth to make the sound bigger and tried to take it an octave lower. She had it.

Finally, the animals gave up trying to open the shutters and left the roof. The sound was less scary as it got farther away, but it was strange how it came and went, got closer and farther. It seemed like whatever was making the sound was swinging above the cabin from one side to the other. That's when Mama figured out what it must have been: some type of monkey.

"Maybe they're called nightmare monkeys," Mama thought. "They sure sound like nightmares."

In the morning Mama asked a man who worked at the hotel about the sound she had heard.

"That sounds like the howling monkeys. They only come through the resort about once a week or so––you got a real treat!" he said.

"A treat?" Mama said. "Do they ever break into people's rooms?"

"Only if they have food in there," the guy said. "But if the shutters are closed properly, they really can't get in. It'll make them pretty mad though."

"Well, that explains last night perfectly," said Mama. "Thank you."

23. Sickness

Now Dave was back in Los Angeles, and Papa was back in Nicaragua. Papa, Mama, and Anders were on a shopping trip in Managua. Papa had brought a tankless hot water heater with him from the United States, and he needed to get parts to install it.

They decided to spend the night at Ken's house. It was a large, beautiful, Spanish-style house with tile floors. Anders loved Ken's house because it was full of people. There was Irma, a live-in housekeeper, Alex, Ken's assistant who was always coming and going, a young entrepreneur from Spain who was staying in one of the bedrooms, and a musician who was staying in another bedroom. Many other people were there throughout the day, working on Ken's different business ventures.

Mama and Papa tossed and turned all night, and when they woke up, they felt like they had not slept at all. First thing in the morning, Papa went to the bathroom and vomited. He crawled on his hands and knees back to bed and told Mama that he felt terrible.

"Can you get me a glass of water?" he asked. Mama didn't feel well herself, but she got up to get Papa a glass of water. She walked to the kitchen. She felt a little dizzy and nauseated.

"Oh no," she thought. "I'm sick too."

In the kitchen Mama saw Irma. Mama tried to smile and say good morning, but she was starting to feel disoriented. Irma took one look at her and knew something was wrong: Mama's face was completely white.

"Go back to bed right now," Irma said.

Mama was in a daze and was still trying to get Papa's glass of water, but she was feeling increasingly ill and desperate to lie down. She mumbled the single word *water* to Irma and left the kitchen.

As Mama was walking down the hallway toward the bedroom, she started to feel like she was melting. She heard Irma cry out, and then everything went black.

Mama had fainted. She had fallen face-forward toward the hard tile floor, but before her head had hit the floor, a man named Juan had caught her. Mama woke up to find her knees on the ground and her upper body being held just off the floor by Juan. When he saw that she had regained consciousness, Juan let her go. Mama did not try to stand but instead crawled to the bedroom.

She got in bed with Papa. Irma brought water. Papa was moaning. Mama and Papa couldn't do anything but lie in bed and moan. Never in their lives had they felt so violently horrible. Their whole bodies hurt. Neither of them could think very clearly. Ken came in to check on them.

"Get Anders out," Mama managed to say. Then she used every bit of strength she had to say to Anders, "Don't touch me, honey. I love you, but I am so ill. I

need you to stay away from me and Papa today. I'm so
sorry." Mama knew that Anders would be well cared
for and was grateful that Ken, who was both
competent and thoughtful, was there to take over.

That whole day Mama and Papa lay in bed.
Papa got up a few more times to vomit. Mama vomited
as well. They both had horrible diarrhea. Ken brought
waters and Gatorades. Mama and Papa couldn't keep
anything down. But worse than that was the way they
felt. They lay in bed, unable to sleep, unable to think,
not well enough to read or even watch a movie. They
just wanted quiet and dark while they lay there and
dealt with the intense pain they felt in every inch of
their bodies.

By evening Mama and Papa were conscious
enough to carry on a conversation. Mostly they talked
about the horror of what they had felt that day. They
still kept Anders at arm's length hoping that he would
not catch whatever it was they had. They went through
everything they had eaten, trying to figure out what
had given them food poisoning. They thought it might
have been what they had had for dinner the night
before, but then it turned out that both James and Nate
at the farm had gotten sick, too. They thought maybe it
was something everyone except Anders had eaten at
the farm, but then they heard that their neighbors had

gotten sick, too. Three days before their illness, their neighbor Trinio had come over to visit.

"Some type of flu then. Some special tropical one," Mama concluded.

The next day Mama and Papa were wiped out. They stayed in bed the whole day. There was no more pain; they were just exhausted from the illness.

When she was well enough to walk around, Mama found the man who had caught her when she fainted.

"I just wanted to say thank you! I would have cracked my head open or lost a tooth if you hadn't caught me! Thank you so much!"

"It was nothing," Juan said. "Glad to help." Mama never saw him again, but she was always grateful to him.

24. Saving and Spending

Now the summer was ending, and it was time to head back to Los Angeles.

"I am not sad to go," Mama said.

"What we're doing is so hard," Papa said. "But it will be epic."

"If we succeed. Sometimes I think we're crazy. I don't know if we can do this," Mama said.

"We may fail," Papa said. "But right now, we're not committed. We're just … seeing if we want to do this. We can pull out anytime."

Papa had been saving his money since he was a teenager. He got a job working for tips at a golf course when he was fourteen. He washed dishes all the way through college. He didn't make much money back then—never more than the minimum wage—but he saved almost every penny.

Papa believed the proper savings rate for a young person was eighty percent. This meant that if he made a hundred dollars, he saved eighty. After working and saving for ten years, Papa had enough money to buy a house. At twenty-four years old he began making rental income every month on that house. As Papa continued learning about money and working, he made more money. But he never spent more. He saved.

Mama met Papa when he was twenty-two years old. He drove a car that didn't have an air conditioner; he slept at his uncle's house for free, and when he outstayed his welcome there, he slept at his grandmother's house for free; he owned only two suits for work and wore them over and over until they were threadbare; he wore rags when he was not at work; he never went to the movies or bought music, never went out to eat, and never took vacations that cost money; he only did free yoga; he had gone to community college and then a state school and had not taken out a single loan for his education.

Dating Papa was not as much fun as dating men who weren't so obsessed with saving, but Mama knew the sacrifices Tom was making would pay off, and she thought his ability to make those sacrifices and delay gratification was attractive.

Mama had also started working at a young age. She was eleven when she began working for her teacher after school. She worked for that teacher for four years and then got a job washing dishes and

146

eventually cooking in her high school's dining room. She worked as a tutor during college, making a good salary. But Mama saved nothing. She spent her money on books and supplies for school, clothes, music, meals out, movies, trips to Europe, extravagant birthday parties, gifts for friends, and numerous purchases for her immediate family. When Mama met Papa, she not only had no savings, she owed tens of thousands of dollars in student-loan debt.

Mama learned quickly from Papa's inspiring example, and by the time they had known each other five years, she had not only paid off all of her student loans, she had also saved an impressive amount of money.

It was hard for Mama and Papa to spend their savings and spend it on something so wild and possibly crazy as their dream of having a family farm with a beautiful home where they could breathe air free of pollution, drink water free of chlorine and fluoride, enjoy a night sky free of light pollution, eat food free of chemicals that was grown in soil that improved each year rather than got depleted—a place that would make them healthier just by being there rather than sicker, as Los Angeles was doing.

"Pull out?!" Mama said, "But this is our dream!"

"Having a farm is our dream," Papa said. "But it doesn't have to be in Nicaragua. We could have bought a farm closer to Los Angeles like you wanted, a farm that was already built instead of building one from scratch! Doing this is only my dream if you and Anders are happy here too."

"I wouldn't say I am happy here, but I am not unhappy. I am fine. And in the end, living here, as hard as it is, is more *interesting* than living in Los Angeles. I'm a sucker for interesting."

Papa smiled. "Do you like it here, Anders?"

"I loooooove it here!" Anders said.

"All right, it's settled. We won't cut and run. But we will go spend some relaxing months in Los Angeles enjoying good food and easy shopping and our friends and continuing to explore the possibilities of this place…."

25. Worms and Phone Calls

Now they were back in Los Angeles. Papa went to work before it was light out. Mama read in bed while Anders slept.

When Anders woke up, they went to the kitchen. There, Mama made scrambled eggs with mushrooms for breakfast. Anders had eaten mushrooms many times, but today, when she and Anders sat down to eat, he stared at his eggs for a bit, and then he picked one of the mushrooms out of them.

"This a worm," he said seriously to Mama.

"Oh?" Mama said.

"I looooove worms," Anders said, popping the mushroom into his mouth. Mama laughed. Anders picked all the mushrooms out of his eggs and ate them.

"Soooo yummy. Looooove worms. Thank you, Mama, making me worms."

"You're welcome, Anders," said Mama.

After breakfast they did the dishes and then went about picking up each room of the house. They made the bedrooms and the bathrooms look nice. When they were working on the office, Anders took Mama's smart phone and said to Mama, "Let's call Papa. I need tell him it would be really helpful if he came back home."

"Sure," said Mama.

Anders called Papa on Mama's phone, something he had figured out how to do before he was a year old.

"Papa?" said Anders. "Hi, when you come home?"

"Hi Anders!" said Papa happily. He loved calls from Anders. "I have only been at work for a few hours. I won't be home until much later."

Anders hung up the phone and handed it to Mama. "Anders," Mama said, "it's a custom to tell people you're done talking before you hang up the phone. I usually say *goodbye* before I hang up the phone."

"Okay," Anders said. He took the phone and called Papa back.

"Hello?" said Papa.

"All done," Anders said and then hung up again. He handed the phone to Mama. Mama laughed.

"That was clearer," she said, making a mental note to play phone games with Anders later to work on his phone manners. "Now that we are done picking up the house, we need to go to the grocery store. We have two choices: we can leave now, or we can leave in five minutes. You can decide."

"Nooooo," Anders said. "Those aren't *my* choices. My choice is to stay home."

Mama was surprised at this reply. Giving young children two choices was a classic parenting strategy that was supposed to work until Anders was much older. He wasn't even three yet!

"Oh," Mama said, "Hmmmmm. Well . . . I wanted to make a tasty dinner tonight, and to do that I need to buy some food. I want you to be happy, but I also want to make a tasty dinner. What should we do?"

Anders thought about this for a minute and said, "What you want, Mama? I love you, want you be happy."

"I would like to go in five minutes," Mama said.

"Okay. I'm ready in five minutes," Anders said.

26. Anders Is Mad

Papa was busy with a project at work for a few weeks, and Anders saw little of him. One day, Papa said to Anders, "I'm going to leave for work early again tomorrow. Just one more week, and then I will be done with this project, and we can spend more time together again."

Anders was upset. "You wanna go to work—I might hit you! I hide your car keys you can't go!" he said.

"Oh Anders," Papa said, "you feel so mad! Do you want me to hold you? Sometimes when I am mad, what I really need is to cry."

Anders ran to Mama.

"I want Mama hold me!" Anders said.

Anders buried his head in Mama's lap.

"I wanna hit him!" he wailed.

Mama hugged Anders while he cried and said over and over, "Wanna hit him! Wanna hit him!"

"You miss Papa," Mama said, holding him tight. "You feel sad. It's okay to feel sad."

Anders clung to Mama for a few minutes more and then the feeling passed, and he raised his head with a smile.

"I wanna eat Papa 'cause I love him and I want him to be my friend!" he said. Anders ran to Papa.

"I want to be your friend too," Papa said. "I'm so glad you didn't hit me. Even though you wanted to. You are very strong!"

"I'm gonna eat you!" Anders said, starting one of their favorite games.

"Ahhhhhh!" said Papa, pretending to scream and run away as Anders chased him.

27. Third Birthday

Now it was October. Mama said, "Anders, your birthday is coming up. You are going to be three years old! What do you want to do to celebrate?"

"I want to dig!" Anders said.

"At home or at the beach?" asked Mama.

"At home!" said Anders.

"Done, we will celebrate your birthday at home. And what about for food? What would you like to eat?" Mama asked.

"Pesto pasta!" Anders said.

"Done," Mama said. "If we are having pasta for lunch, what do you think of steak and eggs for breakfast?"

"Yummy!" Anders said.

"And what about for dessert?" Mama asked.

"Pumpkin cookies!" Anders said.

"We can do that," Mama said. "But we make pumpkin cookies all the time. If you want, you can have a sugary dessert. We eat healthy most of the time so that we will live long, healthy lives. But on our birthdays, I think we can eat whatever we want, because no matter how healthy we are, we are going to die anyway."

"Then … chocolate cookies," Anders said, remembering the cookies Mama made for Lane, Papa's business partner, every year on his birthday.

"Done," Mama said.

"And are there any friends you would like to come over and dig with you on your birthday?" Mama asked.

"Truman!" Anders said.

"Truman can't come," Mama said. "His family is out of town.

"Oh," Anders said sadly. Then he said, "Eric! And Andrew! And Rob!"

"Okay," Mama said. "Anyone else?"

"Nathaniel," Anders said.

"Okay," Mama said. "I can invite all those guys but … they're grownups. Are there any kids you want to come dig with you?

Anders thought about it for a minute. "No," he said.

"Okay," Mama said.

On the day of Anders's birthday, Papa and Anders went to the store and came home with six large bags of sand. They poured the bags into the sandbox that Papa had recently made for Anders in the backyard. Now, with the six new bags of sand, the sand box was more like a sand mountain. The pile of sand was taller than Anders was. Anders's eyes were big and happy looking at it.

"I've never seen a happier three-year-old," Mama said.

"Happy birthday, Anders," Papa said.

Anders dove at the pile. He climbed to the top. He sat there, cross legged, for a long time just touching the sand and letting it run through his fingers. Then he dug little pits and talked to himself while he played a game.

Mama and Papa sat nearby.

"This is my favorite television show— watching Anders play," Mama said. "There is nothing more beautiful than children happily playing."

After a while Anders climbed down from his sand pile, gathered up his construction machines, and climbed back up.

Soon the guests arrived. Everyone ate pesto pasta and chocolate cookies. Then they just hung out in the backyard and took turns digging with Anders. It was a lovely, low-key afternoon.

It was October in Los Angles, which meant it was ninety degrees out, so Anders was only wearing boxers.

"He actually wanted to be naked, but since people were coming over, I asked him to wear boxers," Mama said.

"You guys are such hippies," Rob said. "I couldn't do it. I would be so embarrassed if my kid were running around in boxers when there were guests in the house."

"But you're all close friends of ours!" Mama said, not seeing any problem with the situation.

"Rob," Papa said, "let me explain. Roslyn doesn't get embarrassed by anything. One day, we were at brunch with my family. Anders was almost a year old, and he was just starting to eat solid foods—before then he had only nursed. We were at a restaurant, a fairly nice one, and Anders was trying out some different foods. I think he was having some berries. He was super new at eating, so pretty much every time he ate, he would gag. Roslyn had told me that that was how babies learn to eat, and if you let them learn to eat on their own and gag in the beginning when they are learning, they won't ever choke on food later. She says it's all pureeing things that creates the choking problem in the first place. Anyway, the problem is that for everyone who doesn't know these things, gagging looks like choking.[7]

"So, Anders is sitting there, gagging on pretty much everything, and all of my aunts and my grandmother are basically having heart attacks.

---

[7] See *Baby-Led Weaning* by Gill Rapley PhD and Tracey Murkett.

They're watching this baby eat, and they think he's going to die. They're all freaking out. And I'm stressing out because they're all freaking out, and Roslyn hasn't even noticed. She's smiling and talking to everyone, and telling them about how babies need to gag, and it's all fine. But it doesn't matter. They're all panicking. I don't think they believed her. They thought Anders was choking, and Roslyn was allowing it. So, I'm like, 'Roz, do you see that everyone is really freaking out? I don't understand how you can sit there cool as a cucumber!' And she looked around at everyone's panicked faces, and she smiled and was like, 'Oh guys, this is *not* the craziest thing you're going to see me do as a mom.'"

Rob started laughing. "That sounds like Roz."

28. Classes

"Anders," Mama said one day, "now that you are three, you are old enough to take classes if you want. Are there any classes you want to take?"

Anders thought about it for a minute, and then said decidedly, "I want take a class in airplanes."

"Oh," Mama said, "What do you want to learn about airplanes? Do you want to build them or fly them or look at them?"

"I want to fly them," Anders said. "Real airplanes. Not toy airplanes. Real ones. Yeah, that's my class. That's the class for me."

"Well, you can definitely take that class when you are older," Mama said, "but right now they would not let you, because you're not big enough. The classes that they have for kids your age are more like swimming, dancing, painting, music, fighting, and gymnastics."

"What's gymnastics?" Anders asked.

"Gymnastics is somersaults and climbing and jumping. Dance and gymnastics are great classes to take because they help you have a stronger core, which will mean less back pain when you are older. Dancing is especially good, as you will want to know how to dance when you get older—it's not just good exercise but a valuable skill. I have also noticed that out of all the different sports, dancers usually have the most beautiful bodies. There are also classes in numbers called math classes. Those are great because you have to learn all about numbers before you can learn about money, and money is an important thing to learn about for your survival."

"How about . . . all the classes?" Anders suggested.

"You could do that," Mama said, "but let's pick a few to start with. What would you like to try first?"

Anders decided on gymnastics and math. Mama spent some time researching on the internet and reading reviews of nearby classes. Soon they headed out to try the classes.

For the math class Mama had chosen Kumon. Anders tried out a Kumon class nearby and did not like it.

"That's too bad," Mama said. "I know it's a really good program. Maybe the teacher at that location was bad. Let's try a different location next week."

The next week they tried out a different Kumon center, but Anders still did not like it.

"Okay," Mama said, "let's not do Kumon right now. Let's try it again when you get a little bit older."

"Like three and a half," said Anders.

"Sure," Mama said, "we can try again when you are three and a half." Sure enough, when Anders tried Kumon again when he was three and a half, he loved it and signed up for the class.

For gymnastics Mama took Anders to the highest-rated gymnastics class in the area. The class was held in a large room with a high ceiling. Soft mats covered the floors and there were fun-looking things everywhere. There were bars on which children could climb and hang, balance beams on which they could walk, and trampolines on which they could jump. In one corner there was even a ball pit! Anders wanted to run around and climb and jump on everything he saw, but he and the other children were told to sit in a circle. The instructor went around the circle until, one by one, all the children had introduced themselves. Then he went around the circle again until, one by one, all the children had said their favorite color.

Mama watched Anders fidget. He didn't want to hear people's names or favorite colors! He wanted to climb, jump, and bounce! Eventually the instructor had all the children get up from the circle and skip to the balance beam. There they were told to line up. This took a while as the children were very young. Finally, the children got to walk across the balance beam. They each got to go once, and then they got back in line. Once they had each gone a second time, the instructor had them all get back in their circle on the floor.

Mama was shocked. The class was half over, and the children had done almost nothing that involved moving their bodies and getting exercise. When the class was over Mama asked Anders what he thought about it.

"I hated it," Anders said.

The next week Mama took Anders to a different gymnastics class, but it was similar to the other class, so he did not like it either.

The following week they tried a third gymnastics class. It was the same problem at all three classes—lots of circle time, lots of quietly waiting in line, and little time moving their bodies. Anders was frustrated because the gymnastics equipment looked fun, and he really wanted to learn how to do the things he had seen the older kids do, but he did not like the classes at all.

"What about a private class?" Mama suggested. "Then you would be the only student in the class, and maybe you would get to learn more of the things you are interested in learning."

Anders thought that sounded like a good idea, so the next week he had a private lesson. Finally, he had a gymnastics class that he liked.

29. Cavities

Anders was now three years old, so it was time to go to the dentist for his first cleaning. Anders had been to the dentist before, for quick checkups, but he had never had a cleaning.

The dentist Mama and Papa liked and had been going to for years was named Dr. Joseph Sarkissian. His office was in a town called Glendale. He was one of only two dentists in the entire county of Los Angeles who was holistic. Being a holistic dentist meant that he thought dental problems were connected to the health of the patient's entire body.

"I evaluate the whole person, not a set of teeth," Dr. Sarkissian said. He was a gentle, soft-spoken man who was kind and patient with children. Anders loved him.

Mama and Anders walked into Dr. Sarkissian's office. He had a large fish tank filled with interesting and colorful fish. Anders went to look at it. Mama checked in with the receptionist.

A few minutes later the hygienist, a woman named Liz, told Anders she was ready for him. Anders and Mama followed her to a small room that had a large chair in the middle with many lights and gadgets surrounding it. Liz asked Anders to sit in the chair. He did, and then she pressed a button that made the chair move so that Anders was lying down. Then she raised the height of the chair. Anders giggled whenever the chair moved.

"You like that," Mama observed.

"Yes," Anders said. He watched Liz curiously. She picked up a scraper tool and reached her hand toward his mouth.

"Open wide!" she said.

Anders turned his head away.

"It's my body! I get to decide what to do!" he said.

Liz looked at Mama, unsure of what she should do.

"You are right, Anders," Mama said. "It's your body, and you get to decide. Do you want Liz to give your teeth a special cleaning?"

"Yeah," Anders said.

"Oh, what are you needing then? Are you needing her to ask you before she touches your mouth?" Mama guessed.

"Yeah," Anders said.

"He's used to people asking him before they touch him," Mama said to Liz.

"Ahhhh," Liz said. "May I put this in your mouth, Sir?"

"Yes!" Anders said. He turned towards her and opened his mouth wide. Liz gently went over every tooth with her scraper tool, cleaning off any plaque she found.

When Liz was done cleaning his teeth, Dr. Sarkissian did an inspection of Anders's teeth.

Dr. Sarkissian told Mama that in the six months since he had last seen Anders, Anders had developed eight cavities. Mama was distraught. She worked so hard to provide her family with healthy, nutrient-dense food, and she brushed Anders's teeth every morning and night. He had never had a cavity before. It made no sense that he would suddenly have eight!

Mama talked to Dr. Sarkissian for a while about what might have caused the cavities. Then they talked about fillings. Dr. Sarkissian said that because Anders was only three, he would have to put Anders to sleep to fill the cavities. Mama asked if they could wait until Anders was older to do the fillings, and Dr. Sarkissian said that that would depend on how fast the cavities worsened.

When they were driving home, Mama told Anders, "You know how, in Nicaragua, I was having everyone drink Gatorade to make sure we didn't get dehydrated or heatstroke?"

"Yeah," Anders said.

"Well, it turns out Gatorade is bad for you. As bad for you as soda. I'm so sorry, Anders. I try so hard not to get tricked into making bad decisions, but I got tricked. In Nicaragua, we should drink water with lime juice and salt, not sugar and food coloring posing as a healthy drink."

"It's okay, Mama," Anders said.

Mama bought a book on healing cavities naturally and read it in one day.[8]

"Anders," she said, "this book says that your body can heal your cavities or at least stop them from getting bigger if you stop eating sugar entirely for three months and take cod liver oil and high vitamin butter oil every day. Would you like to try that?"

Anders liked the idea, so Mama bought the vitamins. It took a week of practicing with larger and larger-sized vitamins, but by the end of the week Anders could swallow the adult-sized cod liver oil pills without any problems.

There were not many dietary changes that Anders had to make: the book recommended a diet similar to the Weston A. Price diet, which was almost identical to how the family ate already. There would be no cookies for a while, even pumpkin cookies made with maple sugar, and no fruit for a while either, but Anders was fine with that to fix his teeth.

---

[8] *Cure Tooth Decay: Heal and Prevent Cavities with Nutrition* by Ramiel Nagel.

So dedicated was he to helping his teeth that Anders went to birthday parties and eschewed having any cake. One time, Mama came home, and his babysitter told her, "I had a bag of cookies in my purse, and I offered Anders one. He said he would love one, but then he asked if it had any sugar in it. I said it did, so he said, 'Nope. I'm not eating sugar right now.'" Mama was blown away by Anders's dedication and self-control.

For three months Anders didn't have even one bite of sugar, and he took his cod liver oil every day. When Anders went back to Dr. Sarkissian, he was told that the cavities were not getting bigger, and that some had even hardened. "With that kind of dedication, you can probably wait until you are older before getting the fillings," Dr. Sarkissian said.

Anders ended up getting the fillings slowly, one or two every six months, starting when he was six years old. By that age he was able to sit through regular filling appointments with only topical anesthetic.

30. Reading

Mama disliked almost all books for young children. She did not like books that confused them about the nature of reality, like books with magic or cats that talked. She thought confusing young children in that way was disrespectful and potentially damaging to their intellect and self-esteem.

Just the other day Papa and Anders had peed on a tree in the backyard, and Papa had said, "The tree says, 'Thank you!'"

Anders responded, "Papa, trees don't talk. But they do use the vitamins from our pee."

Mama loved how clear and confident Anders was about reality, and she did not want to mess that up, but she did want to read to him more. Mama decided to try reading to Anders from *Little House in the Big Woods* by Laura Ingles Wilder. It was a true story about real people. It was a chapter book and perhaps a little advanced for a three-year-old, but because Anders had never been to daycare or preschool and had spent most of his life around adults, he had a much more developed vocabulary than most three-year-olds, so Mama thought it could work.

It was a huge success. Anders enjoyed the book so much that he asked Mama to read it to him often during the day as well as at bedtime. They finished the book in less than a week and began the sequel, *Little House on the Prairie,* shortly thereafter.

One day after they were finished reading Anders said, "Mama have baby in belly?"

Mama said, "Are you wanting a sister like Laura has?"

"Yeah," Anders said. "I want sister."

"Yeah," said Mama. "Well, I don't have a baby in my belly, honey."

"When you want baby, Mama?" Anders asked.

"Our life is too crazy right now," Mama answered. "But maybe next year will be a better time."

"I want baby now," said Anders.

"The problem is that babies are a looooot of work," Mama explained.

"I help you! I work hard. Work sooooooo hard," Anders said.

"I am sure you would help a lot, Anders. But babies also need a lot of attention. And you still need a lot of attention. I would be so sad to not give you the attention you need," Mama said.

"That's okay. You can give baby 'tention. I give baby 'tention too! Babies so cute. Teeeeny tiny. Grow up SO fast," Anders said.

"Yeah," Mama said. "I wish I could give you a baby brother or sister right now. They are really cute."

Mama had spent a few years reading extensively about hunter gatherers. One thing she had learned was that hunter gatherers spaced their children three to six years apart. To space children closer than that was considered dangerous to the mother's health. It was also believed that a child born so soon would be unhealthy in some way as the mother did not have time to replenish the store of nutrients she needed to grow a healthy baby.

In the early 1900s a dentist named Weston A. Price noticed that many more children had crooked teeth in his time than in the past. He traveled the world studying the phenomenon of crooked teeth (and other things as well) and concluded that the main cause of crooked teeth was diet. The loss of ancient child spacing wisdom was part of that.

In the past women had nursed their young until they were three to five years old. Nursing for that long made evolutionary sense as all other mammals nursed their young for a third of their childhood, meaning that if it took that mammal three years to grow up, the mother nursed it for one. If it took that mammal nine years to grow up, the mother nursed her young for three years. Humans take twelve to sixteen years to grow up. It makes sense that humans used to nurse their young for three to five years.

A few hundred years ago, nursing went out of style, and women began weaning their children at very young ages. Child mortality skyrocketed. Because nursing makes a mother less likely to get pregnant, and women were no longer nursing, they started getting pregnant more often. This led to centuries of women getting pregnant before their bodies had properly healed from their last pregnancy and death in childbirth became common.[9]

---

[9] Today the World Hleath Organization recommends that couples wait for at least two to three years between births in order to reduce the risk of adverse maternal and child health outcomes. Studies by the United States Agency for International Development suggest that an interval of three to five years might help to reduce these risks even further. See *Report of a WHO Technical Consultation on Birth Spacing* Geneva, Switzerland 13–15 June 2005.

In the United States now, dying in childbirth or childhood is rare, but most children will have crooked teeth.[10] There are many theories about what is causing the epidemic of crooked teeth. Lack of nutrients is just one of them, but Mama saw no reason not to control what she could—which was her own diet and how closely she spaced her children.

"If I died tomorrow," Mama explained to Anders, "my body would decompose into soil, dirt. Humans are just plots of soil than can walk and talk. We know that to grow healthy plants, we need healthy soil, soil that is full of nutrients. The more nutrients the soil has, the more the plant will have. The more nutrients the plant has, the healthier and stronger it will be. If I want to grow a strong, healthy baby, I must first tend the soil in which the baby will grow, which is my body.

In the meantime, Mama decided to get Anders a baby doll and a stroller, in case he wanted to pretend he had a baby sister. Anders, however, being a typical

---

[10] See *Prevalence of malocclusion and orthodontic treatment need in the United States: estimates from the NHANES III survey* by WR Proffit, HW Fields, and LJ Moray on PubMed.com

little boy, never played with the doll. It sat unused in his room except sometimes as an item to be tossed in the air or pounded with a hammer. The stroller turned into a wheelbarrow that he used to transport piles of dirt and tools around the backyard.

31. Hitting

An indoor playground had just opened at the mall. Mama thought this was a good idea for days when it was too hot and sunny to take Anders to the park, so she and Anders went to check it out.

The place was called Giggles and Hugs, and when Mama and Anders first walked in, they could not believe how noisy and chaotic it was. Children ran around, talked, and laughed. Intense electronic pop music blared on speakers around the room.

"Hear that music?" Anders said, "I think it's about tractors crashing!"

Mama agreed. She looked around. The walls were a mural of rolling green hills and blue sky with pictures of unicorns, castles, knights, dragons, and pirate ships. One side of the room was a restaurant with pink tile floors and white tables and chairs where children and adults sat eating pizza and chicken fingers. The other side of the room had soft gray flooring and a large play structure that looked half like a castle and half like a pirate ship. Children climbed, jumped, and hung on various parts of the play structure.

To one side of the play structure was a large screen with a game console and chairs where two older children sat playing video games. In the restaurant area a television played a popular cartoon movie that a table of children stared at while eating.

Mama knew instantly that she would never return to this place, but for today, she paid the entrance fee and Anders removed his shoes. They went through a small gate into the room. Mama sat down at a table. Anders stood near her for a moment, staring at the chaotic room and trying to decide where to go.

Soon, Anders ran off to play. There was a toy car that children could climb into and pretend to drive. Anders went to check it out. Mama watched him, annoyed that the car had a face on it, but confident Anders already knew that cars were not alive. Mama watched Anders for a bit and then took out her book.

Twenty minutes or so later, Anders ran up to Mama and climbed onto her lap. He was crying. He was saying something, but Mama could not understand a word of it, so she held him until he was done crying. Then she said, "Anders, can you tell me again what happened? Because I didn't understand when you told me before."

"I wouldn't let her have the car, so she hit me!" Anders said.

"Oooh," said Mama, "where did she hit you?"

Anders showed Mama a spot on his arm.

"Go talk to her, Mama!" Anders said.

"What would you like me to say?" Mama asked.

"Not to hit me ever again!" Anders said.

"Okay, we can go talk to her," Mama said. "Which girl was it?"

Anders pointed at a girl who was at the top of the play structure. She looked about the same age as Anders.

"Let's wait until she isn't on the play structure, so she is easier to talk to," Mama said.

Anders watched the girl intensely for quite some time.

"I'm thinking about hitting her," he said.

"Oh," Mama said.

"Yeah, I want to hit her," Anders said.

"What do you think will happen if you hit her?" Mama said.

Anders thought about it but did not answer.

"If you hit her, maybe she will cry. Or maybe she will hit you again," Mama said.

"Look, Mama! There she is! Let's go talk to her!" Anders said.

Mama and Anders walked up to the girl, who was now close by. Mama knelt down to talk to her; Anders hid behind Mama.

"Hi," Mama said, "Anders just wanted to talk to you because he felt really sad when you hit him."

Anders peered from behind Mama's back and looked at the girl. Tears came back into his eyes. The girl looked at him. Tears came to her eyes too.

"Anders might feel better if you said you were sorry," Mama said helpfully.

"Sorry," the girl said. She walked around Mama to Anders and gave him a hug. Anders smiled. Then she smiled, and they both ran back to the playground.

Mama marveled at how little she had had to do. A lot of the time, children experiencing conflict did not need her to be their policemen or their judge, they just needed her to be their newscaster, giving words to their feelings and needs, and then they did the rest.

32. Nicaragua Trip Three

Now it was December, and the family was headed back to the farm in Nicaragua. Again, they had twelve suitcases full of stuff, and again Mama and Anders would stay for three months while Papa would travel back and forth for work.

Not much had changed at the farm since their last trip. Nate still worked as the farm manager, James still worked as the cook, Brava, who was much bigger now, still worked as the guard dog, Anders's frog friend still lived in the bathroom sink, and Max and his team would be back to do building projects while Papa, Mama, and Anders were there to oversee them.

A new addition to the farm was a chicken Nate had purchased. It slept in a tree outside the little one-room building Nate lived in. Nate had hoped it would lay eggs that he could sell to Mama, but unfortunately, if the chicken was laying eggs, Nate had no idea where.

Some things would be better on this trip. James had requested help in the kitchen when Mama and Anders were visiting, so now a woman named Dolores would come every day to do the laundry and keep the kitchen and bathroom clean. Mama was hoping to raise hygiene standards at the farm. She had gotten the stomach flu at least once on every trip to Nicaragua so far, and she did not want that pattern to continue.

Mama had brought kefir grains—little colonies of kefir bacteria that looked kind of like cauliflower—to put in the milk they bought from their neighbor. The milk was fresh and was from cows that lived in a pasture and ate grass, but Papa had watched the neighbors milk their cows and had noted that the people milking did not wash their hands or the cows' udders before milking. That was not a sanitary way to milk, so Papa didn't think the milk was safe to drink in its raw state.

The kefir grains would turn the milk into kefir, which would be safe to drink because fermented milk products have such powerful bactericidal properties.[11]

Mama had loved kefir for many years as she had been lactose intolerant when she was younger and cured herself by drinking kefir. Now she was curious to see whether what she had read about kefir's other curative properties was true as well.

---

[11] See *The Untold Story of Milk: The History, Politics, and Science of Nature's Perfect Food: Raw Milk from Pasture-Fed Cows* by Ron Schmid, ND

Mama did not get to find out on this trip, however, because James liked the first batch of kefir she made so much that he drank the whole thing.

"It had a chewy, cheese-like part at the end," he told Mama excitedly that morning. "But it was so good anyway! I loved it, and it made my stomach feel amazing! When can we make more?"

"We can't make more," Mama said. "The chewy, cheese-like part you ate at the end was the grains. You ate the grains."

Another welcome change at the farm was that Mama didn't have to go to town to buy fruits and vegetables anymore: a pickup truck that served as a little store had started coming to the farm every Sunday.

The best change was that, because the portable air conditioner had broken, Papa had agreed to buy a wall unit. The wall unit cost three times as much as the little portable air conditioner had, but it could make the room seventy-five degrees or even cooler, unlike the portable air conditioner that never got the room below eighty-five. The new wall unit also did a great job at dehumidifying the room, which meant the room smelled less musty. The new air conditioner made life at the farm much more bearable for Mama.

The worst change was that the door that Carlos had made had aged poorly. There were spaces in the pieces of wood where there previously had not been any. The same thing had happened to the furniture Erick had built.

Mama asked Erick what had happened, and he said the wood had shrunk. Mama asked why the wood shrank, and he said the wood he had used was green.

"Why did you build with green wood?" Mama asked.

"It was the only wood available for sale," Erick said.

"But if it was green, why didn't you just tell me it was green and hold off on building anything until the wood was properly dry?" Mama asked.

"You didn't say to do that. You said to build stuff," Erick said.

Mama was super frustrated. She didn't understand why Erick had done what he did. She knew there was something cultural that she was missing, some miscommunication, but she didn't know what it was. "What a sad waste of time and money," Mama thought, near tears.

To Erick she said, "In the future, please don't build with green wood. I would rather have no door and no furniture than a door and furniture that become ugly six months after you build them."

After asking more questions, Mama learned that it was not possible to buy dry wood in Nicaragua. There were no stores that sold already-seasoned wood. Whenever Erick needed wood, he would order it from a nearby person with wood to sell. Only then would the tree be cut down. When wood was delivered to the farm, it was always freshly cut. If Mama wanted things to be built with dry wood, it would be necessary to order the wood six months to a year before Erick built anything with it. That meant Mama needed to have a place to store wood while it dried properly.

"If that's how it has to be, that's how it has to be," Mama said. She instructed Erick to stop building immediately and instead to focus on ordering enough wood for a year's worth of furniture projects. Papa would be building a workshop soon, and the wood could be stored there while it dried. In the meantime, Erick could fix the door and the furniture with the shrunken wood and help Max's team with what they were working on.

33. Trinio's Shack

The big project of this trip to the farm was the workshop. Papa needed a workshop where he could store all the tools and supplies that he needed for the farm. Erick also needed a workshop where he could build things.

Max's team cleared an area of the forest not far from the rancho and hand-dug a foundation about fourteen feet wide, twenty-four feet long, and five inches to three feet deep (the building was to be built on a slope). They built a cement floor and a wood frame. Then they needed to take down Trinio's old shack, so that they could reuse the wood for the walls of the workshop.

Before Papa bought the land, it was owned by a man named Ebinor. The caretaker of his property was called Trinio. Trinio was a short, thin man who, until recently, had lived in a shack on the top of the small hill on the property. The shack was one room and had a dirt floor. Trinio did not have a trash can or do dump runs, so there was trash all over the floor of the shack and all over the hill surrounding the shack.

One of the first things Papa did when he arrived at the farm was to have all the trash picked up, even the small pieces, which was difficult for the workers to understand. Trash maintenance required a constant effort with the workers, as it was not their habit to look for a trash can but rather to throw trash on the ground. The trash around Trinio's shack had built up so much over the years that Trinio lived there that now, whenever the rain washed away an inch of soil, new trash was revealed. This wasn't just unsightly; it was dangerous. Trinio liked to drink beer, so a significant amount of the trash was broken glass that had been beer bottles.

Trinio told Papa that he had actually moved from his shack about a year before Papa had bought the land because an overwhelming number of scorpions and snakes had come to the area. Trinio thought they might have been drawn by the trash, which provided ample hiding places for them. Trinio's baby daughter got stung by scorpions so many times that his wife insisted that they leave the shack. They had moved into a shack on the property next door—on Lillian's land.

Sure enough, when Max's team was taking down Trinio's old shack they found—and killed—over a dozen scorpions. They also saw one snake, but it slithered away before they could get it.

Papa, Mama, and Anders celebrated the day the shack came down. The shack had been the ugliest thing at the farm, and it was nice to see it go. The hill looked nicer without it, and now Mama could envision how the duplex could be extended there.

The problem was that Mama had been reading architectural books by Christopher Alexander, who believed that beauty was not in the eye of the beholder but rather an objective fact, a quality that made people feel happy, alive, and inspired. Christopher Alexander argued that beauty wasn't a luxury but a necessity for humans. He said that beauty begat beauty and ugliness begat ugliness and because of that, each building, and especially the first building built in any given area, had to be beautiful. Otherwise, it would be almost impossible to create beauty.

The duplex was ugly. Mama had done her best to make the interior look as nice as possible, but the shape of the windows and the doors were ugly. Beautiful rectangles, Mama had learned, had width-to-height ratios of 1:3, 2:3, and 1:9[12]. Rectangles, in general, looked best when divided into thirds. The windows, doors, and rooms of the duplex were all rectangles that had ratios closer to 4:5. They were almost squares, but not quite, which was not attractive.

"Your job," Papa had said, "is to envision what to build next. We need more rooms and a dining hall. How can we add on to the duplex in a way that makes it beautiful?"

"Christopher Alexander says we should tear it down and start over," Mama had replied. "He says that I will fail to create something truly beautiful if I start with the current duplex, but . . . I can't tear it down. I'm just going to do the best I can."

Papa agreed.

---

[12] The actual ratios are $1{:}\pi$, $2\pi{:}3\pi$, and $1{:}3\pi$.

With the wood from Trinio's shack, Max's team and Papa built the walls of the workshop. They added a metal roof and a door that locked securely. Now Papa had a safe place to keep his tools and supplies, and Erick had a place to build and to store wood while it dried.

34. The Pool

They had returned from a shopping trip to Managua, and Anders kept asking to go back. Every day, he asked Mama if they could please go to back to that hotel in Managua where they had stayed. Mama questioned Anders about this, trying to figure out what exactly Anders was wanting. Was it the older boys at the hotel who played with him? Was it the beauty of the hotel? Was it the food? Eventually, Mama discovered that Anders's desire to return to the hotel in Managua was about the pool.

"One day, we will have a pool here at the farm," Mama told Anders, "but I am afraid that will not be for quite a while. We have many other things to build first."

The next day Mama and Anders went to Juigalpa to run errands. Juigalpa was a small city about forty minutes from the farm that had a MaxiPali. MaxiPali was the Nicaraguan version of Wal-Mart. At MaxiPali Mama saw an inflatable plastic pool. It was small, only six feet by nine feet, and Mama didn't know if there was enough water at the farm to fill it, but she bought it anyway, thinking about how hot it was at the farm. If they could fill the pool, it would be a wonderful way for Anders to cool off. Also, Anders had not been enjoying his five-gallon-bucket baths, so Mama hoped that the pool would be a fun way for Anders to get clean.

When she got back to the farm, Mama blew up the pool, and Nate pumped extra water from the dam to fill it. When it was ready, Anders got in immediately. It was the perfect size. He swam around and played in it for a long time. He was happy. Mama came over and put her feet in the water.

"It's freezing! How are you swimming in that?!" Mama asked.

"It's not cold to me," Anders said.

Two kids who lived on the farm across the highway, Yesnir and Jesslyn, had been coming over periodically to play with Anders since the previous trip. Now they came over every day.

Yesnir was nine, and his sister Jesslyn was three. They were polite, well-behaved children who were beautifully healthy. They had strong bodies, wide smiles, and bright white teeth. They did not wear shoes. They walked through the prickly, stinging-ant infested grass and, if they were stung, barely flinched as they picked the ants off themselves. They loved the pool as much as Anders did. Mama thought there was not enough space in the little pool for a nine-year-old and two three-year-olds, but the kids didn't seem to mind at all.

There was a lot of shrieking and laughing when the children swam. They invented many different pool games. In Anders's favorite game, Yesnir would pretend he was drowning, and Anders and Jesslyn would save him. Anders did not speak a lot of Spanish yet, though he was learning it rapidly. The other children did not speak a word of English, but they managed to communicate and have a great time.

Anders never got tired of the pool that winter. For the rest of the trip, he got into the pool once an hour every hour over the course of every day. He was usually in the pool before breakfast, and, after being in it on and off all day, still insisted on taking one last dip in the dark right before bed.

35. Christmas

"Anders, Christmas is tomorrow!" Mama said. "See this tree?" Mama pointed to the small, decorated, and lit Christmas tree about two feet high that sat on the floor in a corner of the room. "Tomorrow when you wake up, there will be presents under this tree."

"Presents?!" Anders said, his eyes big and excited.

Mama took three stockings out of a suitcase she had stored under the bed and placed them under the tree.

"Anders," Mama said, "these are stockings. Tonight, after you go to sleep, I am going to put some surprises in the stockings. Then when you wake up in the morning, you will find them. Does that sound fun?"

"Yes!" said Anders.

"Even though I am going to fill the stockings, and the presents under the tree are from Mama and Papa, in our culture we pretend that the stockings were filled magically in the middle of the night by a man named Santa. So, when you get the surprises in your stocking, you can say, 'Look what Santa brought me!'"

"Okay," said Anders. He thought this sounded like a very fun game.

The next morning when Anders woke up and saw the presents and the stuffed stockings, he was excited. He ran straight to the little tree and stuck his hand into each stocking. Mama showed him which stocking was his, and he excitedly took out a new tape measure, a new screwdriver, and a small box of maple candy. Then Anders opened the presents "Santa" had left for him under the tree. They were games: Memory, Jenga, and Twister.

When all the presents were open, and the stockings were empty, Anders wanted to pretend to go to sleep and wake up and have there be presents again.

"Let's play Santa!" Anders said.

Mama put his new screwdriver, his tape measure, and his box of maple candy back in his stocking. She put the games back under the Christmas tree. Anders pretended to wake up.

"My stocking is full!" he said. "There are presents under the tree! It's magic!" Anders ran to his stocking and emptied it. "Again?" he asked Mama.

"How about we do it one more time and then we do it again tonight when you really go to sleep?" Mama asked.

"Okay!" said Anders.

For the rest of the week Mama put different small toys in Anders's stocking every night while he slept. They were all toys that Anders already owned, but that didn't alter the excitement for Anders. Every night he checked his stocking to make sure it was empty. When he woke up and it was full, it felt magical—even though he knew Mama was one filling it.

36. Nighttime

It was nighttime. Mama lay in bed reading. Anders climbed up the ladder-like, solid-wood headboard of her queen bed and then jumped from the headboard to the mattress. It was quite a big jump! He giggled with glee. Three more times he climbed the big ladder headboard to the top and jumped to the mattress. The fourth time he climbed up, he stopped when he got to the top. "I'm thirsty," he said.

Mama put her book down. "I can get you some water," she said.

"Don't worry," Anders said. "Don't get up. I can come down there. I can meet your needs."

"Oh, that's great, then I can keep reading," Mama said, picking her book back up.

Anders climbed down the headboard, put on his headlamp and his boots, and left the room. Now he was on the patio. Brava was sleeping right outside their door. Anders stopped for a moment to pat her head and tell her that she was a good dog. Then he walked to the edge of the patio. Brava went with him.

He shined the flashlight on the grass, checking to make sure there were no large toads or tarantulas, and then ran down the small hill to the rancho. The rancho was still a rough building with three walls and a floor of wooden planks that bent as they were walked on, but the sink now had hot water in addition to cold. Near the table where the family ate meals was a low counter where filtered water and glasses were kept. Anders got himself a clean glass and filled it with water.

Beyond the rancho, Anders could see the light on in the bedroom he shared with Mama. He could see the light on in the farm manager's bedroom farther away. Besides those two lights, there were no lights to be seen except for the stars. It was very dark. But Anders was not afraid of the dark, even out here in the jungle. Perhaps it was because Mama and Papa loved the dark so much. They raved about how good it was for their hormones and their sleep. Anders loved snuggling up to Mama at night and trying to see his hand in front of his face. He could never see it here at the farm, even though his eyes were wide open. It was hilarious!

Many people were impressed that Anders was not afraid of the dark, but Anders had not yet been exposed to fiction, had never had a nightmare, and had no idea why other children were afraid of the dark. He wasn't just not afraid of it; he thought the dark was beautiful. It made the stars sparkle like diamonds. Anders loved the stars. And diamonds.

Anders finished his water, put his glass in the sink, and climbed the hill back to the patio. He stopped outside the bedroom door.

"Here, Brava," he said, patting his hand on the spot outside the door where Brava slept. "Sleep here." Brava licked his hand and lay down on her spot. She was a good dog. Anders patted her on the head and went back into the room.

He smiled at Mama and, taking on the air of a caretaker, informed her, "I am going to come check on you and see if you are tired and need to go to sleep."

He walked over to where Mama was and put his hand lovingly on her arm. With concern in his voice he asked, "Are you ready to go to sleep? Are you tired?"

Mama smiled. "I am tired. I would be happy to go to sleep," she said. "Are you ready to go to sleep too?"

"No, I'm not ready," Anders said with authority. "I need to do more work, jumping. How about you go to sleep, and I jump, then I get my needs and your needs!"

"I love that idea, Anders. I really like it when you think of ways for us to both get our needs met," Mama said.

"Yeah! We both get our needs met!" Anders agreed.

Mama put her book away and closed her eyes. There was no way she would actually be able to sleep with Anders jumping on the bed, but she was happy to relax and listen to her little boy having fun.

"I'm glad you are getting your fill of bed-jumping," Mama said. "Soon you will weigh thirty pounds, and after you weigh thirty pounds, you will be too big to jump on beds anymore."

"Yeah," Anders said, seriously. "Every day my body grows some more."

Anders climbed and jump, climbed and jumped, climbed and jumped. Then he was done. He cuddled up next to Mama, and they drifted off to sleep.

Afterward

To see what the farm looks like now, go to TheCacaoFarm.com.

If you enjoyed this book, consider checking out my blog — RoslynRoss.blogspot.com. Also, please consider leaving a review on Amazon. I am a self-published author, so every review matters!

Videos

I have created a playlist for this book on my YouTube channel, *Roslyn Ross*. The playlist is called *City Family Farm Family*. Here is a list of the videos included and a short explanation for them:

How to NOT treat children (or anyone)

> In this video you are invited to "meet" Mama and Papa in (hopefully) an entertaining way.

Anders Keeps His Legs Straight to Help with Diaper Change (2m)

> Due to nudity, I cannot show you an entire RIE diaper change, but here is the end of one. Anders, at two months, helped me with his diaper changes by keeping his legs straight.

Reading (7m)

In this video I show you how I read to Anders before he was two years old. I read few baby books to Anders.

Anders Says Yes (1y)

Anders's trademark behavior as a toddler was that he said "yes" to pretty much everything, and he said it in a wonderfully enthusiasic way. This video captures that.

Anders at the Playground (1y1m)

This is how a baby raised with RIE techniques moves. They are so careful and graceful!

Anders Puts Apples in the Blender (1y5m)

Anders and I spent a lot of time in the kitchen. Here is one of my favorite videos showing that.

Anders Hammering (1y10m)

Hammering was such a big part of Anders's toddler-hood that I overlooked taking videos of it! This is the only one I have.

Happy Birthday (2y)

This video captures nicely just how excited Anders was about his second birthday.

Anders Sings Happy Birthday (2y1m)

This video captures nicely just how excited Anders still was about his birthday a month later.

Anders Makes Eggs, part 1/3 (2y2m)
Anders Makes Eggs, part 2/3 (2y2m)
Anders Makes Eggs, part 3/3 (2y2m)

This series of videos shows Anders making scrambled eggs and sausage for breakfast when he was two-years-old.

Traveling

This video shows Tom at the airport carrying an insane amount of baggage during one of our trips to Nicaragua.

2013 at the Cacao Farm

In this video Tom walks down the driveway of our newly purchased land. You can see how dry and damaged it is. At the end, you can see the rancho being built and Trinio's shack up on the hill.

Anders Mixes Cement (2y4m)

This video shows Anders immitating the grownups around him.

Anders Plays the Harmonica (2y4m)

This is one of the only videos of the farm that I have from its early years. In this video you can see Anders with our friend Andrew who was visiting. They are sitting outside the fourplex.

Anders at the Renaissance Faire 1 (2y6m)
Anders at the Renaissance Faire 2 (2y6m)
Anders at the Renaissance Faire 3 (2y6m)

City Family Farm Family

Anders at the Renaissance Faire 4 (2y6m)

> This series illustrates the chapter about the Renaissance Faire.

Shopping with Anders 1 (2y11m)
Shopping with Anders 2 (2y11m)
Shopping with Anders 3 (2y11m)

> This video shows how careful Anders was pushing the shopping cart. Many people stressed out when they saw him doing this, but he never crashed.

Thank You Cards (3y)

> The person receiving this thank you card only saw the scribbles, but there were thoughts behind them!

Having Fun at Ikea (3y)
Anders and Ikea Furniture (3y)

> Anders is slightly older in these videos than he was in the chapter about Ikea in this book, but they are the only Ikea videos I have so I wanted to include them.

Roslyn Ross

Pumpkin Cookies Recipe

Ingredients

1/3 cup pumpkin puree, patted dry with a paper towel

1/2 cup maple sugar

8 tablespoons (1 stick) unsalted butter, softened

1 large egg

1 tsp vanilla

1/4 tsp ground cinnamon

pinch ground gigner

pinch ground cloves

pinch ground allspice

1/2 cup white spelt flour

1/2 cup whole grain spelt flour

1/4 tsp baking soda

1/4 tsp baking powder

1/4 tsp salt

Instructions

1. Adjust an oven rack to the middle position and heat the oven to 350 degrees. Line a large baking sheet with parchment paper.

2. Put the pumpkin puree into a bowl. Press gently with a duble layer of paper towels until the towels are saturated. Throw the towels away. Repeat this until you have only 1/4 of a cup of pumpkin puree.

3. Add the sugar and butter to the pumpkin puree. Beat until creamy, either by hand or with a mixer.

4. Add the egg, vanilla, cinnamon, ginger, cloves, and allspice. Mix.

5. In a separate bowl mix the white flour, whole grain flour, baking soda, baking powder, and salt.

6. Gently add the wet ingredients to the dry ingredients and mix until combined.

7. Place 1-inch balls on the parchment paper. Flatten them to approximately 1/3" thick.

8. Bake for 8-10 minutes.

Anders's Reading List

       I did not spend a lot of time reading to Anders before he was 3, partly because it is so hard to find reality-oriented books for young children and partly because I don't enjoy reading books over and over, which is what young children generally want. Rather than reading a story before bed, I would turn out the lights, cuddle up with Anders, and we would talk about our day.

       Despite this, Anders still became a total bookworm and read at a twefth grade level by the time he was nine years old.

Under 1
Baby Faces by DK Publishing
Freight Train by Donald Crews

Age 1
Baby's First Book of Birds and Colors by Phyllis Tildes
Bathwater's Hot by Shirley Hughes
Big and Little by Margaret Miller
Brush, Brush, Brush by Rookie Toddler
Cat by Matthew Van Fleet
Colors by Pantone
Dog by Matthew Van Fleet
First 100 Machines by Bright Baby

In the Town All Year Round by Rotraut Berner
Montessori Number Work by Bobby and June George
Montessori Letter Work by Bobby and June George
Montessori Shape Work by Bobby and June George
Moo by Matthew Van Fleet
My Big Animal Book by Roger Priddy
My Big Train Book by Roger Priddy
My Big Truck Book by Roger Priddy
My Five Senses by Margaret Miller
See, Touch, Feel by Piddy Books

Age 2
Apple Farmer Annie by Monica Wellington
Brush, Brush, Brush by Rookie Toddler
Construction by Sally Sutton
Different? Same! By Heather Tekavec
Dig, Dump, Roll by Sally Sutton
Henry and Mudge by Cynthia Ryland
Jet Plane: How It Works by David Macualay
Montessori Number Work by Bobby and June George
Montessori Letter Work by Bobby and June George
Montessori Shape Work by Bobby and June George
Let's Read and Find Out Science series, level 1,
        Various Authors
My Fire Engine by Michael Rex
Pelle's New Suit by Elsa Beskow
Our Animal Friends by Alisce and Martin Provensen
The Greatest Gymnast of All (MathStart) by Stuart J.
        Murphy
The Truck Book by Harry McNaught
Truck Driver Tom by Monica Wellington

Anders's Workbook List

I have listed the workbooks in order of difficulty. The first seven were not available when Anders was two, but they are an even better place to start than the book with which Anders started. I used them with Anders's brother, Henrik, and they were a huge hit.

If Anders (or Henrik) really liked a workbook or seemed like he wasn't ready to move on, I bought a new one and had him do it again — mastery of skills is much more important than rushing. Henrik did some of the initial sticker books three times. On the flop side, if Anders (or Henrik) was bored with a workbook and wanted to skip ahead to the end (and clearly able to do that level of work) I allowed him to skip ahead – – I do not believe in unnecessary repeition.

If a book is too hard, I put it away and try it again three to six months later.

For workbooks, we use Pencil Buddies Short Thick Triangle Pencils For Kids.

Age 2
Step by Step stickers by Kumon
Vocabulary Sticker Books by Kumon
Counting with Stickers by Kumon

Let's Color by Kumon
Let's Fold by Kumon
Let's Cut Paper by Kumon

Let's Sticker & Paste by Kumon

My First Book of Tracing by Kumon
My Book of Amazing Tracing by Kumon
My Book of Easy Mazes by Kumon

Brain Quest, age 2-3
Brain Quest, age 3-4

Mathematical Reasoning by The Critical Thinking
      Company
Building Thinking Skills, Beginning 1 by The Critical
      Thinking Company
Visual Perceptual Skill Building, Book 1 by The
      Critical Thinking Company
Fun Time Phonics by the Critical Thinking Company

Anders's Puzzle List

These are the puzzles Anders enjoyed which I consider part of his education curriculum.

Age 2
Montessori Nuts & Bolts by Meroco
Math Wooden Number Shape Set with Learning Clock and Lacing Beads by Asher and Olivia
Stack & Sort Board by Melissa & Doug
Wooden Sorting & Stacking Toy by Pebira
Cylinder Blocks by Thoth (monochromatic)
Chunky Puzzle by Melissa and Doug
Wooden Peg Puzzles by Melissa and Doug
Farmyard 2-piece puzzles by Orchard Toys
Head to Tail puzzle by Match it
Wooden Jigsaw Puzzles by Melissa and Doug
Uppercase and Lowercase Alphabet Montessori Style Sandpaper Letters by BleuZoo
Doorbell House by Melissa & Doug
Marble Run Set by Marble Genius

Acknowledgments

Anders — Thank you for letting me read this to you so many times and giving me your crucial feedback, not to mention your enthusiasm.

Tom — Thank you for your support. This book could not exist without you.

Nate & James — Thank you for the memories we share and for being part of this adventure. I hope you write your own books one day. My stories pale in comparison to yours.

Ken & Carmen — Thank you for making this adventure possible, for your friendship, and for the truly endlessly support.

Diane, Abbigayle, Arlo & Ely — Thank you for reading an early draft of this book and giving me your feedback.

George — Thank you for your invaluable feedback.

Cynthia Keller-Bennett — Thank you for your editing services.

Alexander Cohen — Thank you for your editing services.

Made in United States
Troutdale, OR
07/20/2023

11417162R00130